Copyright © 2019 Andy Lingwood

ISBN: 978-0-244-19701-8

The moral rights of the author have been asserted. All rights reserved. No part of this publication may be reproduced, stored in a retrieval system or transmitted in any form or by any means, electronic, mechanical or otherwise without the written permission of the Publisher.

Dedication

I have written this book for my family both those in the UK and Australia, and for myself, and anyone who has been on the same journey or is planning to. This was a voyage of discovery that started when I was thirteen years old, when I found a piece of paper that I eventually realised was an adoption certificate revealing that I was someone else other than the person I had grown up as so far.

Far from being disappointed I was intrigued.

Acknowledgements

Sincere thanks to, Carlie from Pen Friends UK (www.pefruk.co.uk) who proofread the first edition for me and Angela Carless for assisting me with photographs and press releases. Not forgetting all the numerous people who advised, encouraged and insisted I put this into print.

CONTENT

Prologue

One - The Beginning

Two - The Moment of Discovery

Three - Revelations and Tragedy

Four - But in the Meantime

Five - Telling the Family

Six - The Journey Begins

Seven - Welcome to New Zealand

Eight - The Final Outcome

Nine - The Inevitable Fallout

Ten - More Revelations

Eleven - A Rock and a Hard Place

Twelve - In Retrospect

Thirteen – It's Too Late

Fourteen – The Surprises Keep Coming

Fifteen – The Unbelievable Happens

Sixteen – The Pain and the Agony

Seventeen – This Has To Be How It Ends

Epilogue

Family Tree

Prologue

WHAT YOU ARE about to read is an account of my life from the age of thirteen until the present day. A journey that was initially of fits and starts dead ends and frustration. As an adopted child I was privileged in the extreme in that I was selected for adoption by two wonderful, caring and giving parents called Michael and Una.

I grew up in a modest, comfortable home in High Wycombe in Buckinghamshire with my two sisters, Lesley and Caroline and two brothers, Alistair and Duncan. Another brother, Stuart, was tragically taken from us whilst a baby, a victim of cot death. He is however still a part of the family and there is not a single significant event in life that we all experience, when he has not been in our thoughts. Some would say we wanted for nothing as we grew up, but Mum and Dad were absolutely certain that we should learn the true value of life and the trials and tribulations it could bring; experiences that I benefit from now and will pass onto my own children.

The old adage that we will end up saying what our parents said, and start sounding like them, is so true. I will be forever grateful to my adopted parents and I miss my Mum dreadfully sometimes, in particular when I look at all my children as they grow and mature. My parents gave me the start in life that has brought me love, children and happiness.

It all sounds so idyllic and wonderful doesn't it? However, like all real life biographies, I have had my fair share of heartaches and pain. I went through stages in my life where I was bitter and angry and resentful; so I would not and could not be naive enough to say my life was perfect. It would be obtuse of me to document all those events here but they were all relevant and instrumental in bringing me to where I am today. This is the story of my life and my discoveries along the way, there have been highs and lows and a lot of what I have achieved now could not have been done with out the love, support and encouragement of people around me.

This is my story; people who know the story have encouraged me to put this into print, so here you are. I hope it makes you cry and smile and as a result realise that silver linings do exist in clouds in this sometimes troubled world of ours.

Be prepared for a roller coaster of emotions, but enjoy the ride and share in the exhilaration and the disappointment that was my journey.

My birth mother Sally holding me (on the left) and my twin just prior to handing us over to our adoptive parents Una and Michael

One

The Beginning

MY CHILDHOOD WAS NOT, to be fair, that remarkable. I was adopted along with my twin brother in 1963. We were very fortunate in that we were taken on by two generous and caring parents who lived in High Wycombe in Buckinghamshire. They already had a daughter, Lesley who was a couple of years older than us. Mum had always maintained that she wanted at least five children but was told that after Lesley this may not be easy, so the process of adoption presented an alternative. Happily though, Mum's fears and concerns were unfounded and along came Duncan, her second born in 1964, and so we became a family of four. Stuart was born in 1966 and the family of five was complete, however the joy of Stuart was short lived as he died not long after coming into this world. Yet out of so much sorrow there was joy in the form of a baby sister, Caroline, in 1967 and we were once again complete.

My adopted parents Una and Michael

The first few years were pretty uneventful. We all grew up together in a wonderful happy and close environment, surrounded by loving parents and relatives. There were the usual traumas of first days at school; I can recall my first day at Priory Road Junior School quite vividly. I was inconsolable (I can still visualise the classroom in this bleak old Victorian building) and I was led away from my mum in floods of tears. As a parent who has experienced leaving their child at school on their first day, I can now imagine that must have made my mum feel dreadful.

In the Infants' School I was in Mrs Redgrave's Class that was just down the corridor from the canteen. The canteen was laid out with tables and benches and the food was brought in and served from tables at the front, imagine if you will a scene from the Charles Dickens' novel, Oliver Twist. For some peculiar reason, I recall having a penchant for the skin on the custard, whether it is vanilla or chocolate, and if I ever had the impudence to ask for more, I usually got it.

I settled into the routine of school soon enough and from Mrs Redgrave's class it was into Mrs. Haddock's and Mrs. White's and finally into Mrs Jacobs. Mrs Jacobs was a formidable woman to a child of seven and one of those teachers who could put the fear of God into a child just by looking at them. Her speciality was a protracted withering stare.

Corporal punishment was still practiced in schools back then, and even just the threat of it was enough most of the time to keep you on the straight and narrow. School in those early years went by mostly in a blur, and only certain significant events feature in my memory. I vaguely remember on occasion being driven to school but generally we walked, even at a very young age and in all weathers

Imagine asking youngsters and indeed some mothers to walk these days, sadly for some it's all they can do to walk to the car on the drive, let alone all the way to school. I also remember Prince Charles's investiture as the Prince of Wales on 1st July 1969. We were all subjected to what seemed like hours of television, watching something which meant absolutely nothing to your average seven year old. We would much rather have been daubing something with paint, or out in the playground doing something far more constructive instead. Then of course, not long after there was the alleged moon landing on the 21st July 1969. I say alleged to pacify my son Damian, who is adamant the whole thing was an elaborate fabrication. If it was a hoax then millions of children across the world were needlessly dragged from their beds to hear the immortal words 'the eagle has landed' and of course Neil Armstrong making the speech etched in the minds of everybody who heard it, 'this is one small step for man one giant leap for mankind'. A small enough comment at the time, but significant enough to keep people quoting it for years to come and of course talk in the playground the next morning was about rocket ships and spacemen.

I can still remember the playground and playing with toy cars amongst the dirt at the base of the beech trees that lined the school wall. Playing football, skinning knees as a result of having to wear shorts even in the coldest of winters, and being mercilessly teased when I arrived at school one day wearing brown corduroy trousers. They were straight legged and not in the least bit flared, a fashion faux pas worthy of bullying it would seem back in the early 1970's.

I can also remember, and God only knows why, the school hall where we gathered for school assembly. It was headed up by the headmaster, Mr. Tom Evans, a giant it seemed to primary school children. Although he was feared (as headmasters had a right to be then) he was loved by all who knew him both staff and pupils. So it came as a huge shock when he was tragically killed in a road accident one summer on his way to Wales, a couple of years after I had left the school. But I digress. Back to the hall of memories, I apologise profusely for this one, but an enduring memory of the school hall was of pupil's stomach contents. Whenever an unfortunate child vomited at their post during assembly, we were all subjected to the almost instantaneous aroma of cheap disinfectant and the subsequent pile of sawdust rushed in by the caretaker to conceal the offending puddle.

On a much more pleasant note, I remember being enthralled at Christmas with what seemed to a small child, huge decorations and a Christmas tree that always appeared in the last weeks of term. Didn't it always snow at Christmas in those days as well?

I, like a lot of children, remember long sunny summer holidays. As a family we used to travel up to Scotland overnight, all the children laid out and supposedly asleep in the rear of our Austin Cambridge; there were no child safety seats or safety belts in those days. We even used to take along our faithful Golden Labrador "Sandy". How on earth we managed with five children and a Labrador in the back of the car all the way to Scotland is anybody's guess. Scotland was my dad's homeland, in particular Coldstream in the beautiful Scottish Borders. It is located on the River Tweed, and when his mother and father still lived there just across the border from England, we used to arrive in the early hours of the morning and were all bundled into bed, having either been carried from the car or made our own way stumbling sleepy-eyed into the first day of our holiday. Days were usually spent on the beaches or visiting a variety of relatives scattered around the area on various farms, a time and a place that can only be described as idyllic and one of fond memories long since gone.

Just recently, I took my family back to the same area and sought out the very same farms and beaches I encountered as a child. I was delighted to find that even through an adult's eye, the places still held a certain kind of magic. Edinburgh to this day is still by far and away my most favourite city in the world.

As I got older we started to venture further away from home for our holidays, and I was fortunate to have the opportunity to travel to places such as France, Germany, Switzerland Austria and Italy. This was still in the early 1970's so foreign travel was still in its infancy. We laugh about it now but whenever we were abroad it always seemed to be me that was ill or injured in some way.

We were staying on Lake Garda in Italy one year and whilst sitting by the pool (quite happily minding my own business) I was struck on the ankle by a stone that had been launched, as far as we were aware, from a catapult. I

sustained an injury that left me with a scar that I still bear to this day. I can still remember mum being absolutely
horrified when we sought treatment and the doctor asking permission to put stitches in with a needle and thread. Luckily for me this didn't happen, but the injury meant I had to miss out on certain activities. My brothers and sisters all got to go on some large trampolines, I was not allowed but I can still hear my dad saying, 'don't worry Andrew, I will bring you back another time'

You know what? I am still waiting now and I even used to remind Dad from time to time of his promise (much to his amusement). But I suspect my turn will never come on those trampolines, rather too old now methinks.

I was also banned from entering water of any kind be it pool or lake, so whilst the rest of the family took to the water I was left to amuse myself dejectedly on the beach. Dad once again came to the rescue and duly arrived on the beach with a blow up rubber dinghy with oars saying that if I was not allowed in the water there was nothing to stop me being on it.

My ultimate claim to fame with regard to holidays abroad, has to be our mammoth trip across Europe in a

Danbury converted Volkswagen camper van, which for some curious reason was called 'Zebedee'. I think it had to do with the fact that we being children used to have to jump in and out of it.

It was the kind of vehicle that had a roof that extended upwards, allowing two beds to be assembled in the roof space, as well as the rest of the interior being laid flat to make further beds with curtains all round. It was equipped with its own sink with a tap you had to pump to draw water out of a canister underneath, and a cooker secreted under one of the seats, powered by a large gas cylinder. One assumes now that kind of set-up would from a health and safety point of view would be completely unacceptable, however for us children it was just so much fun. In addition to the space within 'Zebedee', we also had a large awning-style tent that attached to the side, so affording even more space.

The van was even featured on television, as part of a documentary about a band of travelling troubadours, known as the Unicorn Group. They were under the direction of the very talented Peter Levers, and performed passion plays (a dramatic presentation depicting the passion of Christ) locally in High Wycombe. They even produced a series of long playing records LP's. and my family and I were members of the group so immortalised on vinyl somewhere. The television programme was a Yorkshire TV production called 'Stars on Sunday' and 'Zebedee' was shown with hordes of kids leaping out of it, all very strange really, but it was the 1970's after all and at least I got to be on television.

One of our trips took us to Europe which took us across France into West Germany, visiting Bonn where friends of the family, Ursula and Rolfe lived. They lived in a brand new house that was built with a cellar, a sign of the times it would seem. It was built that way in order to provide shelter in case of a Nuclear War. Possibly a prudent move considering West Germany's proximity to Russia, although at the time the SALT II (Strategic Arms Limitations Talks) were well underway, having started in November 1972. To my delight our transportation whilst with Ursula and Rolfe, when not in our camper van, was in two original Herbie style Volkswagen Beetles, one blue and one orange. In those days, Bonn was a modern city with lots of new buildings, and we visited various parts, although I cannot remember exactly, I am certain we would have visited

Beethoven's birthplace at Bonngasse 20; where he was born in one of the attic rooms in December 1770.

It was in Bonn that I became aware of a problem with a tooth, but I said nothing to my parents despite the pain. To this day I can't recollect why I didn't just tell them.

Perhaps it was due to my track record to date and an element of fear of what would happen as a consequence. In hindsight it was probably the most self-centred thing I could have done when you consider we were staying with the only two people who could have probably helped arrange local dentists to sort the problem out.

We travelled to Switzerland and over and through the Alps via the St. Gothard Pass, This was the old route before the new road tunnel opened up in 1980 and which reached a height of 6,935 feet (2,114 metres). Imagine the exhilaration for us children having left the warmth and sunshine at the bottom and slowly making our way up into the mountains. The old Volkswagen camper vans only had a 1300cc engine and fully loaded with two adults, five children and associated luggage it made it hard going, but on reaching the summit we found snow.

Snow in the middle of summer was breathtaking and from a child's perspective had to be seen and touched to be believed. We had seen it before from a distance on mountains, but now we could touch it and run about on it and - as we soon discovered - get very cold as well. We were only dressed in shorts and t-shirts and so it was that we gratefully all clambered back into our camper and started our descent into Italy. Downwards was somewhat faster than the slow climb we had just endured. The roads were the type seen in that classic film 'The Italian Job' with bends that seemed to go on for ever and sweeping vistas with breathtaking drops, sometimes on either side.

Whilst in Italy we visited Pisa and its world famous leaning bell tower, the building of which started in 1173. As a result of two long interruptions, it took about two hundred years to build.

We carried onwards, stopping overnight in various campsites along the way to the city of Florence. In Florence we wondered at the marvels of its well-known son Michelangelo, and the Ponte Vecchio 'Jewellers Bridge' which spans the river Arno. Next on our journey, Rome and our final destination, where we were to set up camp for a week. We visited the Coliseum, The Forum and The Vatican; after all we were in one the oldest cities in Europe. It just oozed culture and even someone as young as me couldn't fail to be awestruck.

However, all the while I was secretly nursing excruciating toothache, which as we headed north again was to quite literally change the course of the holiday. On reaching the South of France and the Principality of Monaco, my mouth suddenly swelled up and it was then that Mum and Dad realised I had a huge abscess under my tooth. My dad, to his credit, drove overnight from the South of France back to Calais via Paris (where Dad confessed to getting ever so slightly lost, which found him scratching his head somewhere in the middle of the night in the centre of Paris). However some friendly locals obviously realising his predicament, stopped to assist and with their excellent command of the English language, much to Dad's relief, suggested he follow them and after a short while managed to get him back on to the right road and pointing in the right direction for the ferry port. From there it was a quick dash across the English Channel (well as quick as you can be on a ferry bearing in mind this was a long time before the

Channel Tunnel), and then onwards back home to High Wycombe in order to get me and my tooth into a dentist's chair and absolute relief. I am not entirely sure my family have forgiven me yet for having their holiday cut short because of that tooth, but I certainly appreciated Dad's mercy dash that night.

As is usually the way, there were those who influenced me in various ways throughout my life. One of those influences was my dear Auntie Bobs (Roberta). She lived in the suburbs of Selly Oak, in Birmingham, and I used to spend my Easter breaks with her and my grandmother. My grandmother left Scotland and went to live with Auntie Bobs, as it all became a bit much for her on her own following the death of her husband, my Dad's father.

I used to love spending time with both of them; the journey to Birmingham was an adventure in itself as I took the train from High Wycombe, changing at Banbury and having time to take refreshment in the little station café. The café was over the platforms as I recall, with trains passing underneath. They were the old circa 1970's intercity trains (nothing like the sleek, almost stealth like conveyances of today) with separate compartments and hard seats and were incredibly noisy, so the café used to resound with the noise of the passing locomotive and the tang of diesel fumes.

After my glass of milk or orange squash and chocolate bar or bun, it was then onwards to Birmingham watching out for the Bullring in the city centre which signalled journeys end.

My Aunt would meet me at New Street and my holiday would truly start. I remember days out to various locations around Birmingham, usually of a cultural nature like Charlecote Park in Warwickshire. Our mode of
transport was a Renault 4, an ugly vehicle with the gear change being mounted in the dash and which always reminded me of a roller skate with a roof on it.

My aunt was a spinster and never married and she was sadly taken from us by cancer in the 1980's. We did get to spend one last holiday together only this time we were in Crete.

For some reason my mum and dad decided not to tell me that she was already ill before we left something I still find difficult to come to terms with. If I had known, I would have understood why we couldn't do certain trips or why she had been so tired and needed to retire early of an evening. Worst of all was when we went on a trip into the mountains to a small Greek village for an evening of traditional Greek food and entertainment. The wine and ouzo was flowing and I disgraced myself by getting horrendously drunk for the first time in my life; my poor Aunt, who was far more ill than I ever was, had to contend with her inebriated nephew. I was absolutely mortified when I found out far later how ill she had been, and as such have never forgiven myself. I watched her eaten away by the cruellest of diseases in Selly Oak Hospital, and it broke my heart. At her funeral I cried so hard that I vowed never to cry again. I often wonder what she would have made of me now and how I turned out. I hope she would be proud of me and I am certain she would have loved all my children as much as she loved me.

So it was onto Secondary School I failed the eleven plus examination and I found myself being schooled at Beaconsfield Secondary Modern School, Aylesbury End in Beaconsfield, Buckinghamshire. My school career could not have been less spectacular. I was an average student with average grades, except for maths. I hated maths with about as much passion as my mum loved the subject, to this day I will never understand how or why $a + y = z - 4$ etc could have anything whatsoever to do with adding up the daily shopping bill or working out the measurements of a room for carpet.

I never excelled at sports although I did at one point think I might enjoy cross-country running... however it never lasted with the onset of winter, all that running around in baggy shorts and singlet, in sleet, rain and snow with biting winds making it seem more like torture than it already was. We never had the luxury of being allowed to wear tracksuit bottoms to keep us warm; we had to run harder and faster instead.

It was about this time, aged thirteen that I made the discovery that would change my world and send me off on a difficult journey. Retrospectively, the discovery changed my life instantly, although at the time I was not aware of the impact it was going to have on me. My outlook on life though, definitely changed from that day on.

I developed friendships at school but the one person who meant anything to me was my best friend ever, Lynn. As we got older I think I wished deep down that we could have been more than friends. I think I can put that down to the adolescent fantasies of a teenage male, which (quite frankly) was somewhat inevitable by the age of fifteen. By that time I was indulging in my first adventures with the opposite sex, scary but enlightening times.

    I was into motorbikes in a big way and by holding down a job at the local Woolworths in High Wycombe stacking shelves both after school and at weekends, I was able to purchase the first of many bikes I was to own. My pride and joy for 1979 was a three year old Suzuki AP50 in red- I can even remember the number plate- TUD459P.

    Unfortunately after I sold her, I heard she was thrown under a lorry not long after and flattened, all that fettling and care gone to waste. Thankfully the rider was unscathed.

    My love affair with bikes has remained with me and I guess I have had a bike on and off, both new and old, every four years or so since that first one. Currently I am hankering after a Triumph Bonneville, which is a sensible bike to own given my age, too many aches and pains to be scrunched up on a sports bike now.

    However that said I was fortunate in that I survived to the ripe old age that I have, many of my contemporaries didn't.

When I reached the age of seventeen, over one three month period, it seemed like a vendetta was being waged against friends of mine who were being killed and maimed in bike crashes.

One particular was a lad I grew up with called Andrew, who lived four houses up from mine. We spent countless hours in and out of each other's houses, making camps in the local woods and once, constructing a rope swing in the huge weeping willow in his front garden. Well it seemed huge at the time. Because the gardens were on a slope, we were able to swing out and over the pavement that ran along the boundary of the house.

He and his family moved away to Kent and I can remember my mum taking a phone call from his mum, informing us that he had been killed on his bike a new Suzuki X7, which at the time was the bike every teenager who was into bikes had to have, as it was the first 250cc bike to top 100mph. He had misjudged a corner and ridden straight into the front of a bus. It was my first brush with the spectre of death in such appalling circumstances and again a time that had a profound affect on me as well.

It was at Secondary School that the inevitable careers interview loomed, but I was adamant I knew what I wanted to do with my life. I wanted to go into Forestry, so imagine my surprise when my mum said I should think again, because there was no way I would make the grade for the college in Cumbria.

There is no denying I was hurt to think that my mum had so little faith in me. Okay, I thought, how about taking a plumbing apprenticeship in Chesham? No, that was not to be either as it was too far to travel (despite the fact that I had taken to riding a motorbike).

I even succumbed to the Army Careers Office recruiting drive and secured a place with the Royal Electrical and Mechanical Engineers (REME) but mum refused to sign the necessary documents on the grounds that, with the Northern Ireland troubles ongoing, the Army was the last place I was going. My brother meanwhile had signed up for an apprenticeship with a local plant hire company so had his future mapped out for him. I finally decided the only thing I could do was go back to the sixth form and hope to get some O'Levels, but not being the academic success of the family I was probably seriously clutching at straws. And I knew it.

I spent a month of the summer of 1979 in Spain, staying in the small fishing village of El Portet, just a short walk from Moraira. In hindsight it was a time in my life when I was, for want of a better description, on a voyage of self discovery. It was the first time I had spent any significant time away from home, and a time when I was to meet up with a family who would have a significant and enduring influence on my outlook on life. Even when I was back in the U.K. and spending time with them in Meopham, (a village in Kent), I was becoming increasingly aware that there was a different approach to life than the one I had become accustomed too.

I remember the parties on the lawn that encircled the house, the house being constantly full of music and the party being hosted by two of the coolest parents I had ever met. Just recently we have all met up again, twenty seven years on from when I first walked past them sitting outside a small bar on the beachfront. Ian in his pink Lacoste polo shirt and Carin, (who now knows I was somewhat besotted with her- for gods sake I was a hormonal sixteen year old who had just made friends with a lad in Spain who just happened to have a stunning sister!)

Also with them were their younger brothers Gary, Lee and of course their parents, Pete and Jean. It was a strange yet fantastic experience meeting them all again all of us with children of the age we were when we first met. Although we hadn't kept in constant touch over the years, they were never far from my thoughts. Suffice to point out whilst in Spain that once again I was the one who sustained any injuries to be had. First off, chronic sunburn which left me with scars on my shoulders followed by the worst case of food poisoning from eating oysters the day before I flew home.

To round the summer off nicely I contracted meningitis as well, that had to be one of the most frightening times of my life. I woke up and realised that not only did I have the mother of all headaches (which meant I couldn't move my head off the pillow without experiencing excruciating pain) but I couldn't see either. For the next few days I drifted in and out of consciousness, completely unaware of anything, or events unfolding around me. Strangely enough though, the one thing I do recall was a conversation between our two family doctors and my Mum and Dad deciding whether or not I should be moved to hospital.

One of the doctors was unwavering in his opinion that I should remain where I was, because in his opinion the consequences of moving could very well be fatal. I finally recovered and the exclusion zone around the house was eventually lifted.

Returning to school, I lasted about three months before drifting into a trainee engineer's position with a local firm, Sharpenset Engineering, but by then I had already made my mind up that I was going to leave home and join the Royal Navy.

By now, my home life had taken on an air of apathy and despondency, I was at a loss as to what I really wanted out of life and felt no matter what I did I was getting no support whatsoever. My Dad was away from home most of the week as he was now working in Birmingham (staying there as a daily commute would have been too much - this was before the M40 went as far as Birmingham) and Mum was now back full time as a teacher at a local High School.

So I went to the Royal Navy and the Basic Training Establishment at Torpoint in Cornwall. The date was the 21st

May 1980, and I became JNAM D184632B Angus (Junior Naval Air Mechanic) but bitter disappointment was still my mentor and I was home again in about six weeks having broken a wrist following a spectacular headfirst dive off the scrambling nets on the assault course. (I have to say I still completed the course, and it wasn't until the next day that they discovered the broken bone in my wrist.)

By now I was at an all-time low, I thought I had found my niche in life and had just made loads of mates and lost them just as quickly. I was given the option of back classing until my wrist had healed, or leaving, I made numerous (and I am not ashamed to admit it), tearful phone calls home, desperate for some guidance and solace, only to be told that it was up to me to make the right decision. I was a young seventeen-year-old who had been more or less cosseted for most of my young life and here I was alone, hurting, and being told to make a decision that would affect the rest of my life.

Retrospectively, I made the wrong decision of leaving. On the train home I knew even then it was the wrong decision. I think we had just gone through Exeter when I realised my error, but it was too late. Some would say it was fate, because in 1982 the Falklands War came about and had I remained at Raleigh and continued in my chosen career of Air Engineering Mechanic, I would probably have been drafted to the area.

On arriving home I was told in no uncertain terms that I was to find a job and soon. It was under these provisos that I found myself in the world of retail jewellery, courtesy of Messrs F. Hinds Ltd in High Wycombe, under the guidance of a fantastic manager Derek Lewis.

I actually quite enjoyed my three years in the jewellery trade, but again I became increasingly unsettled and was never truly happy with my lot. It wasn't long before the lure of the sea and the opportunity to escape pulled me away from home.

This time I was to be a RO (T) D198161T Angus (Tactical Radio Operator) which meant I would be transmitting Morse code by flashing light and signal hoists by means of flags (Although modern technology also meant sitting in an office environment receiving and transmitting signals by satellite communications).

This time I was in it for the duration, well five years anyway, and yes I had an absolute ball… so much so, I could probably write another book on the subject. I breezed through basic training (after all it was the second time I had done it) and no broken bones this time either.

My best mate was a lad called Rob who was the spitting image of Tony Hadley from Spandau Ballet. He was about three years younger than me; when I joined up again I was now aged twenty.

We both got sent to HMS Mercury near Petersfield, in Hampshire, for our training as communicators. Whenever we got off base we used to drive down to his Mum and Dad's house as they lived locally. It was always great just getting away from the Navy for an evening and returning to 'reality' was a real boost to morale.

His Mum and Dad treated me like one of the family and I will always remember the home grown tomatoes which were absolutely mouth watering. Rob and I were fortunate enough to join the same ship as our first draft; HMS Andromeda. That was when our luck ran out but it affected Rob more than me, possibly due to our different ages.

Our mess deck had its share of bullies and they mercilessly taunted Rob and me. In those days, rightly or wrongly, it was accepted as being part and parcel of life below decks but being punched and kicked and verbally abused became too much for Rob and he applied for a branch change. Rob could have been one of the best tactical communicators in the Navy, he was a natural, but it wasn't to be. After we left the ship, he started on his Naval Regulators course in Rosyth. He excelled and having passed out of the course he and some friends went out to celebrate. Tragically he was killed in a car crash that same night and from that day on I have held those bullies personally responsible for his untimely death and taking away my best mate.

I have never met any of them since, and have absolutely no desire to, but I sincerely believe in karma. I know that all of them were involved in a car accident themselves, which, as I understand it, left at least one of them incapacitated enough to be forced to leave the Royal Navy.

As for me, I became well travelled and apparently undertook a transformation which was in some cases not for the better. I became more and more cut off from home and quite happy, or so I thought. After all, I had nothing in common with anyone at home, leave was an inevitable part of navy life but I was always happier on board ship and being a sailor ashore whether in home ports or foreign.

I even volunteered to be transferred onto one of our relief's, HMS Charybdis, in the Gulf in 1985, when they were a man short in order to stay in the Gulf area for a further six months. I remember receiving a letter from Dad on arrival in Gibraltar one year, which told me quite categorically that I didn't have to live life as I was in order to enjoy it. I didn't know it at the time, but I was on a slippery slope to self destruction. I was virtually becoming an alcoholic, at one point I was taking my morning coffee with a dash of whisky and making sure I was in the pub by opening time. It was only with the timely intervention of friends, that I thankfully didn't slide all the way down the slippery slope.

My former wife and I were married in August 1987 in High Wycombe Parish Church. As you would expect, she wanted the wedding day of her dreams and in her own way she did.

We paid for everything and were on a tight budget, which meant a reception in a community centre with a buffet set out on trestle tables. The honeymoon was a couple of nights away at the Weston Manor Hotel, in Weston on the Green in Oxfordshire. I had intended to go back one day, but in some ways thankfully never did. During the honeymoon, the manager took time out of his day to teach us croquet on the lawn to the rear of the hotel. I had played it before but it was still a lot of fun, after all this was on a proper croquet lawn with the proper equipment being taught by someone who actually knew how to play it properly.

Anyway, back to the arrangements for the ceremony itself. There were no relatives from my side of the family invited to the wedding, despite having enough invitations made to cover all eventualities.

My parents had decided it would be too far for some of them to travel. This was despite the fact that Alistair (who had been married only four years before) had everybody who could make it there, including our godparents from Edinburgh and then some and at his two subsequent weddings as well.

The same applied to my sister, Caroline, at her wedding and my younger brother Duncan. They were both married to their respective partners some years after my own wedding, all were lavish affairs which always left me with a bitter taste in the mouth. I made do with just a small group of friends from the Navy and of course my immediate family.

One of the most poignant moments of the wedding however was the night before when I came home, having met up with my friends for my final drink as a single man. My Mum and Dad met me in the kitchen and dropped the bombshell that they had decided they would not be at the wedding. My response is not repeatable, but it had the desired effect and they reluctantly managed to make it to the church, albeit not as the happy and proud parents of the groom.

However had you ever looked at the wedding photographs you would have noted that neither my mum nor dad featured anywhere. It was their decision and theirs alone. They were not happy about the wedding or who I was marrying and made it very obvious how they felt, ironic then that retrospectively, their decision may have been a sound judgement on their behalf after all.

My former wife's side of the family turned out in force and more than made up for my lack of support. We set out in life without a penny to our name but blissfully ignorant to what the future held.

I always found it hard to forgive my family for what happened in August 1987, after all it wasn't only me it affected, it was my former wife, who's special day it was, ultimately, as it is with any bride and her family and far beyond that, my children, who are now old enough to realise, should they ever get to see them, that there were certain key figures missing from their mother and father's wedding photographs - namely Nan and Granddad. Some are inclined to say I remained bitter about it and have perhaps held an enduring grudge. Perhaps retrospectively it should have been brushed under the carpet a long time since, and I would probably have been the first to admit it. But a wedding is one of those events in life that should be significant and memorable and I have been to many weddings since which are always a constant reminder of what perhaps I should have had that August day in 1987. The inevitable breakdown of the relationship between me and my adopted parents was beginning to show.

That was over thirty years ago now and a key time in my life. My search for my biological parents began in earnest; I knew my family were out there somewhere they just had to be.

There began a period of frustration, information was not forthcoming and what information there was I found difficult to get hold of. In 1991 I went to see Social Services who furnished me with the most comprehensive information to date but it was still not enough. It gave me dates, names and approximate ages of Jill, Clare and Stephen who were my biological sisters and brother, but very little else. So once again the folder of information was put away and I tried to get on with my life. I had my son, Damian, who was born in 1988. With the birth of my son came the untimely death of my adopted Mum shortly after she and my dad moved to Sheffield, taken by the same cruellest of illnesses, cancer. I am thankful to this day that she was able to experience the wonder of her first grand child and will always remember our last visit to the Royal Hallamshire Hospital in Sheffield and her parting words as she said goodbye (unbeknown to me at the time) for the last time, 'your son is a credit to you'. She was in reality an incredible woman, loved by all that were fortunate to meet her throughout her all too short life. This was then followed by a difficult and somewhat painful period in our marriage, which we eventually overcame but had caused irreparable damage.

My young family and I settled in Aylesbury and I finally found my niche in society with the Thames Valley Police as a Control Room Operator. I was based in Aylesbury in 1992 and the job allowed me to utilise certain skills I had developed in the Navy. Tamara came along in 1997 and I was eventually promoted to Team Leader with a move to Milton Keynes, and then finally Operational Supervisor, still based in Milton Keynes. It was then that the final pieces of the jigsaw finally fell into place.

A family holiday in Venice with, from left Una (adopted mum), my beloved Auntie Bobs, Lesley, Me, Caroline, Alistair and Duncan.

Two

The Moment of Discovery

It all began in the summer of 2003, following a family holiday in Scotland, where we had spent a week on the Moray Firth in a little fishing village called Crovie.

Little did I know at that time of the events that were about to unfold, and which would change my life dramatically over the next few months and take me on a trip of discovery to the other side of the world.

Like a lot of people before and after me, I had on occasion visited the Friends Reunited website to look up old friends from school. From time to time though, when curiosity got the better of me, I would also search for the names of the three children who were named on my adoption records. Clare, Stephen and Jill and their surname as it would have been in the 1960's. The usual result was a negative one

However, things were going to be different this time around. I entered Clare's name and surname in the name search but rather than spelling as I usually had, Claire, I spelt it Clare and added the place name of Crawley. I was presented with a few names but only one with any real significance in terms of location, dates and details given but now living in Australia. As you can imagine after twenty years of brick walls and dead ends, I was somewhat astounded and staggered by my discovery.

"Left Three Bridges Primary School and immigrated to Australia with my parents in January 1967. Lived in South Australia until 1987 and then moved to Western Australia where I still live. My husband and I run a small business and I finally went back to England for a holiday in 2000."

I should point out at this stage that although I had been searching and making enquiries over the years, it was only on the odd point in time when I had been prompted by a comment or question.

So what should I do now? Turmoil ensued, how should I deal with this? All manner of questions came to mind. What if she is my sister? Should I send her an email and if I do what should I say? It would be totally unethical to send someone an email saying, Hi I am your brother who was put up for adoption. What if she didn't know about me?

What if she did and didn't want to know me or have anything to do with me? So many questions so many indecisions and so much uncertainty. Finally with my mind made up, I drafted a short email as follows to Clare;

Dear Clare

Just out of interest, was your mother's maiden name Audrey May G***, and your fathers name Raymond L***?

With my finger tentatively hovering over the send button, I finally clicked and away it went. My nerves were in shreds by this time and all I could do now was wait; contemplating what the outcome was going to be. Owing to the time difference with Australia I didn't actually have to wait long, bearing in mind it was early evening in Australia and the reply I received was;

Hi Andy

Yes you are right and I have an older sister Jill and an older brother Stephen

By now I was in no doubt about whom I was emailing. However, I had to be diplomatic… this was a huge step for me. I replied with the following;

Hi Clare

I am doing some research into some past events in my life, mainly due to the fact I turned forty this year. Do you ever recall the name Simon L*** from back in the 1960's when I believed your family lived in the Crawley area of Sussex? If you do remember the names and any significant reasons why, I would be interested to know.

The reply was in some ways disappointing but understandable due to Clare's age when she moved to Australia;

Hi Andy

As I was quite young when we left England so these names don't ring any bells for me. I will ask my sister who is seven years older and she may recall these people. I am interested to know how you had the information about my family as my parents separated when I was three and my dad (who we stayed with) re-married when I was seven. Then we moved to South Australia when I was eight.

Undeterred I replied with two emails, the quest was on and the need to know one way or the other was becoming desperate now. I was due to fly out to Paris for a few days and I was now faced with a dilemma, do I ask outright what I wanted to know or did we keep sending emails back and forth slowly chipping away at each other until we revealed the information we were after in order to satisfy our curiosity. Finally after an awful lot of deliberation I made the decision to reply to the most recent email with the following;

Hi Clare

I was aware your parents had split up in 1963. Without opening old memories that should probably remain closed, are you aware of the reasons behind your parents splitting up? I have to admit I am primarily interested in what happened to and where your mother is i.e. did she re-marry and in the U.K. I feel at this stage I should point out that all of the questions I am asking are purely for my own personal interest. As you were only three at the time of the split, it is entirely possible that your brother Stephen or sister Jill may already have the answer to the question you asked.

And just prior to leaving the house at five in the morning for the airport;

Hi Clare

It is 0430 over here and we are just about to head off for the airport for a short break until Friday. I feel that as you already have your suspicions as to who I may be, that it is only fair I tell you. This is by no means the easiest thing to do via e-mail and it has taken me over sixteen years to finally track you guys down. But here goes. I am Simon L***; I am assuming you are aware of the circumstances surrounding your mum and dads split and that the penny may well have dropped. This is by no means easy for me to tell you as I am sure it is for you to accept. However I feel now I can start to close a chapter in my life that has been left open for so long i.e. my reason for being and where I came from. I leave it with you now and fully understand if you want to take this no further. Kindest regards and thanks for your understanding.

It was a difficult decision, but by the same token an easy one to make, and that had to be made. It was a make or break situation, however it still had me again hovering hesitantly over the send button. After all, I could be about to blow it all and end up ruining everything, but then of course it could also be vice versa. Talk about anguish, but the decision had to be made and with a click of a button everything was suddenly in the balance. What was worse, I would have to wait for another three days before I knew what the outcome was going to be. Very early next morning I flew off to Paris and Disneyland with my mind in a complete whirl of anticipation and uncertainty. Three fun packed days later and I was sat in the departure lounge of Charles de Gaulle Airport in Paris, across the way from me was one of those internet machines you see in all modern airports across the world. How tempting was it to log on and view my emails? The urge was almost overwhelming but I managed to resist and it was just as well I did. I was not prepared for what I was to find waiting for me on our return home. What was waiting for me in my inbox was well beyond anything I could have imagined not one, not two but three emails from the other side of the world;

Hi Andy

I am not really sure how I should start this email, I had a fair idea who I maybe writing to. Do I take it you don't use the name Simon L***? Please correct me if I am wrong, also I feel I need to know what information you have and know. As you must know by now I have been talking to Jill a fair bit over the past few days since I received your first email. She has since rang our mother and passed on all the emails that we received from you. I hope this doesn't bother you, because now it means you may also be opening an e-mail from your mother.

I feel at present I can't say too much more in case as most people say I may 'put my foot in it'. We were all victims of circumstances that we were too young to have any control over, I would very much like to keep in touch, but will leave it up to you to decide if this is the outcome your sixteen year search was meant to have.

The above was from Clare, what more could anyone ask for? I was absolutely elated, after all these years I had a sister who was a part of me, but not only that she was aware of my existence and who had, like me, wondered from time to time what had happened all those years ago.

Hi Andy

I am uncertain if you know where we are but Clare lives in Perth, Western Australia and I live in the suburbs of Adelaide, South Australia. I am arriving in England on Thursday of next week (04/09/03) for the first time since 1967. My husband Ken and I will be staying for a few days in Hampshire prior to doing a tour for eleven days and then staying for four to five days in Manchester before coming back home. Our schedule is pretty tight and I am unsure where you live but if you are interested in meeting up and it can be arranged I would be happy to meet with you. I rang my mother yesterday to tell her about you, she was thrilled, so I am sure you will have had an email from her. Please contact me at this e-mail address to arrange a meeting as I am now on leave.

The second one from Jill was, as you can see, equal to Clare's but with the added bonus of an impending visit to the UK planned in the next few weeks, an extraordinary coincidence.

However further to that, Jill had also been in contact with our birth mother, who it turns out was alive and well, living in New Zealand. Up until this point I had almost given up any hope of locating or contacting her. And so the third email, nothing in the world could have prepared me for this. This was beyond anything I could have ever hoped or expected. Not only was my birth mother alive and well, but she had re-married whilst in New Zealand in the early 1970's. Though the person she married was the man she had met back in the England, my birth father. Incredible, both my birth parents were alive and well, but not only were they alive and well they were in a relationship and had been since my conception until now. However as you can see from the emails, they only thought I was someone who was in contact with their son;

Hi,

Can you help? We are Simon and Ian's birth parents. We have tried to contact them for years. We are more than anxious to find *out about them. Please give them our email address. I am rather intrigued as to who you are. Jill has forwarded your e-mails with regard to me. I can give you all the information you require, but I still want to know why you want this information. Are you in touch with my twin boys? Please feel free to e-mail me. I am known as Sally H****

What follows are the replies I sent to Clare, Jill and Sally;

Dear Clare,

Just got back in from Paris, its one o'clock in the morning, trust me you could not put your foot in it. Yes I want to keep in touch, I never imagined any of this would ever happen, Jill has been in touch and yes she has told me that our mother could be in contact as well. I have had an email from Sally and Ted and will be replying to that later. How I was going to approach the aspect of contacting my mother was always going to be an issue. Problem solved because you have already paved the way for me. I am so very, very pleased and excited by it all; you won't know what it means to me that you have all been so open and understanding about all of this. As you said, we are all victims of circumstance and as babes in arms and children we had very little or no say in how our lives were set out

The information I had was limited and was given to be my Social Services back in about 1990. All I had was Mums name as it was then, and the surname of my father who came from Hove, Sussex? I had your dad's name and of course yours Jill's and Stephen's. The last area you had lived in but no actual address. Simon was the name I was given at my birth by mum and I believe your dad as we share the same surname and what was eventually put on my birth certificate. My adoptive parents changed it after the adoption to Brian Andrew Robert Angus but as you can see everyone knows me as Andy.

And

Dear Jill,

Literally just walked through the door from the airport, its' one o'clock in the morning. I would love to meet up, I start back to work on Monday 1st September and finish for four days on the 5th September at 7am, work shifts! Will not let that stand in the way though, so ring me and let me know what suits you. I have received an e-mail from Sally and Ted Harman, so I will be replying to let them know exactly who I am.

I am stunned and amazed by all of this, never in my wildest dreams had I imagined any of this. I love the internet!!!

Finally, the e-mail that was about to complete the circle of life that started way back in 1963 when my mother gave me up for adoption. As yet I was unaware of the significance and revelations that were about to be revealed as result of all of my findings, but for now you have to understand that this was the moment I had thought about frequently since my initial discovery all those years ago. Contact with the woman who gave birth to me, my reason for being and my very existence.

Hi Sally and Ted

How do you put this in an e-mail? I am not only in touch with your twins, but I am Simon. I was only Simon for the first few months of my life and the couple who adopted Ian and I changed our names. I was christened Brian Andrew Robert Angus from then on, but I am known as Andy to all my friends and family.

I was born in Crawley Hospitals Maternity Unit on the 29th April 1963 at 10:00pm and my twin followed at 10:10pm. This is the information I have so believe this to be correct. Some years ago I made a trip to the hospital just to see where I had been born, something most people take for granted, but I had never seen or known where my birth had taken place. I even ended up taking a photograph of the entrance to the maternity unit.

Please get in touch; this is the best thing that could have happened. I have spent nigh on sixteen years tracking and tracing to no avail. I even registered with the Adoption Contact Register in the hope that someone would make contact. I have scoured the voters register for years. This is just so good. Can I take it that Ted is my father? If he is then this makes all this even better because I was never told anything about my birth father other than his surname being Harman and that he came from Hove. I take it from the e-mail address that you live in New Zealand.

Anyway can I call you mum and dad? This is just incredible, in a week I have spoken to Clare, Jill and now you albeit via e-mail. Speak soon

By this time my emotions were all over the place, in the space of a week I had gone from having four names on a piece of paper from enquiries made back in the early 1990's to having been in contact with two sisters and my birth mother and father. Not only that but I knew my brother was also in Australia, but who was as yet unaware of the events currently unfolding. The following are replies from Clare and Sally, short but poignant, but the content spoke volumes and set me off on a roller coaster of emotions again;

Hi Andy,

Firstly welcome back into our strange mixed up and very spread out family. I think it may be easier all round to speak. If it's ok with you I'd like to call you tomorrow at 6:00pm (Aussie Time.) I am sure this makes it about 10:00am in England? If this is inconvenient, could you let me know when you maybe home? Until I hear from you take care.

Hi Simon,

Your dad and I are so overcome with relief that we found you that I will have to sit down and compose an email with answers to all the questions you have asked.

They had also included an attachment that was to reveal some interesting facts that again most people take for granted, a copy of my birth tag showing my weight and length at birth. Also a photograph of my mother holding both me and Ian just prior to us being passed over for adoption, so the last time my mother saw us, spoke to us or held us. Eventually I also received the following;

Hi Simon,

Well here we are again having shed quite a few tears. We also contacted at least two Adoption Contact Registers all to no avail. Every year on your birthday and of course other times, we have wondered how you were getting on. Now our dreams have come true. Yes we did eventually get married – in Auckland, New Zealand in 1974. We had been together for years before that. As you will see from the e-mail attachment we sent you, it gives you answers as to when you were born. We have treasured those birth tags all this time, together with the photo of me holding you for the last time.

It was unfortunate that I was unable to keep you, but dad was also married. What started out as a 'fling' turned into a full blown romance that we have never regretted. Obviously we are going to have to talk at length, but please ask any questions and we will answer them truthfully. We naturally want to know all about you together with a photo. We have sorted out a couple of pictures of us and will send them through in due course. You may be Andy to all and sundry, but to dad and me, you will always be Simon.

It's difficult to explain, it was then and it is now, everybody in the world who has brothers and sisters and who are not adopted could not possibly understand what I felt at that point. They see their brothers, sisters, mum and dad on a daily basis as they grow up, they fight with them, laugh with them and love them and dare I say take them for granted, understandably because they are there 24/7. They can look at them and see similar traits in their mannerisms and features and know without any doubt they are related always have been and always will be.

I was never able to do that, for years I had known of their existence and could only hazard a guess as to what they looked like, where they were and what they thought and now I was on the brink of discovery. It was an incredible rush of emotions and the journey that was to follow was not always going to be what one would have hoped for.

To close this chapter of discovery here is my email to Sally and Ted, sent response to theirs. At this moment in time I was in a state of exhilaration, life surely couldn't get any better than this. What more could anyone ask for?

Morning Mum and Dad,

Overwhelmed and stunned at the moment, but in the best possible way in the world. You wonder what will happen and how you will react when you finally make contact with the people who gave you the most precious gift of all, life. I have never doubted that you thought about me throughout our lives. It was the same for me, always wondering and hoping against all hope that this day would someday happen. I always understood the reasons why you had to give us up. Although I never knew the full details, I never felt any bitterness about the circumstances, just a quiet understanding as to possibly why. It could not have been the easiest decision in the world to make, just by the very fact you kept the birth tags and photograph tells me that.

There are no burning questions that I need to ask and yet there are so many, forty years is a long time after all. I just have an overwhelming sense of relief that I have found you and that you are there for me still. I guess you have a million and one things you want to ask me as well though.

My biggest fear through all this was that if I found you, I would be intruding on someone else's lives. This has proved not to be the case, both Jill and Clare have been so understanding and supportive, Clare even calls me her brother. I cannot tell you how much that means to me. I am so glad this has happened, this has made my fortieth year so very, very special and complete.

Three

Revelations and Tragedy

HAVING EMAILED CLAIRE BOTH recent and not so recent photographs, the time had come for a phone call to be made. Nerves jangling and heart pounding, contact was made. The most remarkable thing of all was that it felt like the most natural thing in the world. Unlike most brothers and sisters speaking on the phone however, we had over forty years worth of news to catch up on. You can probably imagine the kind of questions that were asked, for example birthdays, marriages, births and all manner of personal questions about each other. Making comparisons to each other's lives and how uncannily alike we all were in certain facial features, mannerisms and particular traits. By the end of what must have been the longest phone conversation I had ever had to Clare, I was ecstatic, we had discussed the possibility of us going out to Australia in the future and all meeting up but no firm dates or times had been agreed. We were acutely aware that Jill and her husband Ken were imminently due to visit the UK so that was a hot topic of discussion as she was going to be the first to forge the link in person.

Jill and I had spoken, albeit briefly, to discuss the itinerary that she and Ken had already in place for their trip, in order to arrange a meeting. Like all good stories, we found the only time we could initially meet was when they were between locations, and we were to meet up at Euston Station.

However, unlike all the best stories of assignations at stations, we did not arrange to meet under a clock wearing red roses in our lapels. We had exchanged mobile phone numbers and would co-ordinate our meeting that way. So it was set, the date 20th September 2003 and approximately time 10 o'clock when we would finally meet. We would seal the bond that had unknowingly been formed so many years previously, but that had been broken temporarily by deeds and actions well beyond our control.

In the meantime I had another date with destiny, and finally, after forty years, I was going to at long last speak to the person who gave me life and gave me the opportunity for my very existence, my mother. I thought my nerves were acting up before my phone call to Clare but this was something else. I actually had to pluck up the courage to pick up the phone and dial the number. I had so many preconceived ideas about the situation that I now found myself in, and in a split second they all pale into insignificance. There is a voice at the end of the phone saying 'Hello my darling' a voice that although strange seems familiar, but you just can't put your finger on it exactly. Although you actually know why, of course you do, how can you not? For me it was somewhat stranger, my birth mother had named me before putting me up for adoption and I was Simon, I had always known this but what I hadn't taken into consideration of course was that my birth parents had only ever known me as Simon and for forty years they had only ever referred to me as Simon.

They would never have known I was christened Andrew, or what my surname was, and now the confusion in their first email became apparent. They had expected an email from Simon, not a stranger with the name Andy and now, rightly or wrongly, who was I to take that away from them? In the fullness of time they would have to adjust.

After all, throughout my life I had always been Andrew or Andy, I was christened with that name; I got married with that name my children and all my friends and relatives knew that was my name. There was the first stumbling block, but one I was sure we would be able to adjust to. So for the meantime, in New Zealand I was known as Simon, but as Andy in the rest of the world.

The 20th September had arrived and it found me devoid of children on a train heading into London, destination Euston and whatever the day was going to bring. My feelings and emotions that day are hard to describe, but I guess a mixture of fear, anticipation and wonder probably sums them up. I was to ring once in London and heading for Euston, in order to ensure that Jill and Ken had made it into London and were on schedule for their connection to Manchester. So I duly arrived at Euston Station and by now my stomach although knot free, was sidling into a state of butterflies.

The phone call was made and I was looking for a small coffee bar at the far end of the station. I can't speak for Jill, but the moment I walked into the bar and my eyes came to rest on a couple in the corner and I just knew, there was absolutely no rhyme or reason to it, I just knew it was Jill. We hugged and tears did flow. To the staff of that coffee bar it would appear to just be people who probably hadn't seen each other in a while, what would they have thought had they known the significance of that meeting?

We remained in that coffee bar and strange as it may seem, I couldn't tell you the name of it, but I bet I could walk straight to it if I had to. After coffees we decided that perhaps lunch would be a good idea, as Jill and Ken's train wasn't for a couple of hours yet. We strolled to a nearby pub, and again I couldn't tell you the name of it. You would think perhaps due to the significance of the day, names and places would be burned into the memory but they weren't.

To be honest there was so much to take in and remember that were so infinitely more important, that names of places just didn't register.

As with Clare on the phone, most of the questions were personal and as we talked we smiled and as we smiled we laughed, it was incredible. Here I was in the middle of London, having lunch like ordinary people with my sister and her husband, the only difference being that my sister had an Australian accent and we had never until this day ever had lunch together. Time slipped away quickly and it was time for the Manchester train. I walked them to the train, having collected luggage on the way. We hugged and said our goodbyes and said we would speak soon; it was to be earlier than I realised.

Later that week on the 23rd September 2003, Jill and Ken caught the train down from Manchester and we spent the day together having a pub lunch. We collected the kids from school so my sister and Ken could meet their 'pommie' niece and nephew, Damian and Tamara. They both took to Jill and Ken immediately, we had one of the best family dinners ever but once again time was against us and it was time to say goodbye again. This time was harder, as even in that short space of time there was a tie that ran deep. I missed her then like I miss her now, but none of us could have realised what an impact that one day was going to have on all of us.

It was a week or so later when I took a call quite unexpectedly from David, Clare's husband. I really felt for him that day, as he had to break the news to me that whilst flying into Hong Kong, Ken had suffered a massive heart attack and had subsequently died on arrival. Even now it brings a lump to my throat to recall that awful day. My family and I were privileged to have met Ken and he will be sorely missed by all. It was a long time before we went back to the pub where we had all had lunch that day, and when we did, Ken quite rightly was the topic of conversation. It was a difficult time for all of us; I had the awful feeling that a tragedy of this magnitude was going to have serious implications on what we had been steadily building over the past few weeks. I felt I had to step back and allow Claire, David and Jill the time to grieve for their loss. I felt like I was intruding and didn't know what to do or say. On the one hand I was devastated and felt a need to share the loss as a brother, but equally I was only to well aware that, despite the blood ties, we had only known each other a very short time.

I made the decision and remained on the sidelines and it was the right decision to make. Clare was fantastic and kept me updated with events in Hong Kong and eventually back in Adelaide. Time is a great healer and eventually things got back onto an even keel. The emails continued to flow between us and by now I had booked the family expedition for April 2004 when I would finally get to meet my second sister. The absolute pinnacle of all of this would be to meet my parents not just my mother as is usually the outcome for most adoptees but my father as well. Suffice to say the next seven months were going to be the longest months of my life.

Jill, me and Tamara

Four

But in the Meantime

AS THE BUILD UP to the trip of a lifetime continued, Clare and I spoke regularly, exchanging childhood experiences and theories surrounding my adoption. As the days passed it was becoming apparent that there were more than a few discrepancies with regard to what I had been told over the years. Sally and Ted were constantly on the phone as I rang them virtually every week to keep them up to date with events in my life. You would think I had a million questions to ask, but they never came up in the various conversations we had over those intervening months, something others remarked upon on more than one occasion. As I pointed out to them though, I just wanted to talk to my mum and dad about everyday things as any son would talk to his mum and dad about.

I guess to some degree I was overwhelmed by everything, so much had happened in such a short space of time. I was on a rollercoaster of emotions going to both extremes, incredible highs when speaking to Clare, Jill and mum and dad, sharing forty years worth of each other's lives, laughing and marvelling at the amazing similarities in our mannerisms, thoughts, feelings and experiences. Just one remarkable coincidence for example, David, Clare's husband had spent the first few years of his life living just up the road from where I now lived, indeed his father was a Police Officer for the very force that I now worked for.

In 2000, Clare and David had been in the UK and had been in Aylesbury, Buckinghamshire the town in which I lived. We could very well have passed each other in the street and never known who we were walking past.

Then there were the inevitable lows; the enormity of the situation and the frustration of not being able to just drive down the road and knock on a door. I was even planning a new life in Australia, or if not New Zealand. I was heading at breakneck speed into a new life with my long lost family and life was going to be perfect. However I was all too soon going to find that life, surprisingly enough, was not as simple as I naively believed it to be.

That said, everybody I spoke to was genuinely happy for me. When I told my story to colleagues and friends, I was astounded by the reactions I received, people shed tears as I told and re-told my story of how I had found my family, even as I shared my experiences I found myself struggling to keep my emotions under control. It was about this time I received some of the best advice I could have been given. My sister Caroline (adopted family) who I had confided in a lot over the past few weeks suggested I should contact Social Services and speak to their Adoption Section and ask about counselling.

Initially I resisted, believing that I didn't need the advice of someone who knew nothing about my situation. Who was it that had spent the best part of sixteen years searching? I had read every available publication offering advice and guidance on how to go about the process of finding your birth mother and what the consequences could be if you did and what could happen when you finally met.

But I couldn't have been more wrong and after some not considerable soul searching, I made the call and in a few days time I was sat in an office with a Social Worker, called Jane, preparing to tell my story once again, only this time to a complete stranger. I was stunned by her response, which was totally unexpected. She pointed out that my situation was virtually unique, as both parents were still together and married.

There were indeed strict guidelines and procedures that would normally be recommended and supervised by Social Services under normal circumstances. I had of course by-passed all this and made contact by way of the internet, not only that but within days I had made phone contact and even met members of my family. Normally this would take place over a period of weeks and months building up to a meeting as and when all parties were happy and comfortable with the situation. However far from being criticised for my actions, Jane for the most, complimented me on the fact that I had obviously done my research thoroughly over the years and was fully aware of what may or may not happen on meeting my birth parents.

She took the opportunity to offer me advice on how I should deal with the actual day I met my parents. She suggested I meet them on neutral territory, for example in the hotel lobby where we were staying and that I should meet them on my own initially, due to the likely intensity of emotions that were probable to be present. All sound advice that I accepted with gratitude but as you will see later on did not necessarily follow to the letter, with hindsight, this perhaps as a result helped lead to some unforeseen heartbreaking consequences.

So how were my family coping with all this? They had been through most of my torment and soul searching over the years, indeed they had been the catalyst that had brought me to where I was today. They had rejoiced with me and supported me in my disappointments throughout our life to date. They had tolerated my jaunts across country when I suddenly felt the need to seek out my roots and understood why I needed to take a photograph of a door to the maternity unit of Crawley Hospital. My former wife unbeknown to me, had sent both my sister Clare and my parents her own e-mails and this is what she said;

A big thank you for making Andy's dreams come true, I did wonder if this day would ever arrive. You have made his life complete in so many ways. Words cannot begin to say how much this means to us all, I am just so glad it has happened. I will be forever grateful for your kindness and understanding when Andy first e-mailed you. I can honestly say I was a little worried about the outcome, but I have no such fears now. Just by what Andy has told me, you and he sound very much alike and you look alike as well. Thanks once again for all your help in bringing his family back together. It's just so wonderful for all of you.

Clare's response to the above was equally caring and understanding

Thank you so much for your kind e-mail. I too was a bit worried about you and your family. This is a big event in anybody's life to say the least. I'm just thankful that Andy had met and married such an understanding person like yourself; you must have gone through many disappointments with Andy during his search. Jill and I had many phone calls last week, because as like Andy we didn't know how much information you had. I am so pleased that he has made contact with both his biological parents. It must be mind blowing for him, but having you there as a stabling influence must be a great help. Next time I ring we'll have to have a chat and you can fill me in on some of the things that dear brother of mine has been up to over the years.

The following e-mail was to my mother and father, it came from the heart and was sincere, so what was to materialize later in the story was somewhat surprising to say the least.

Thank you so much for making my husband the happiest man alive. I have always told him that as a mother myself; you would not and could not have forgotten him. There have been times when he has almost given up hope of ever finding you both. But he persevered and we have the best possible result. I can't wait to meet you both in April. Your son is a very kind and caring man who you will love as much as I do. Once again thank you for being there for him.

My parents responded accordingly and without any doubt or reservations or so it would seem.

What a really lovely email we have just received from you. I don't think we can express just how elated we are to have found our family. It just doesn't seem possible that after all our wonderings of how our boys were doing that we are finally all together. Can't wait until next year – but of course we will have to as we haven't won the lotto. Heaps and heaps of love to you all

What more could anyone ask for? I appeared to have a wife who seemed to be completely accepting of all that was unfolding. She had met me, married me and come to know my family over the years and now I was expecting her to do it all over again with another facet to my family, who, although she was aware of them, like me never imagined she would ever get to meet. Ironic then that despite the above emails, underneath all the written sincerity, there was trouble brewing that would hugely contradict all of the above emails.

Five

Telling the Family

MOST WOULD BE WONDERING by now how the rest of my family in the United Kingdom must have been reacting to my discoveries. Well, it was a mixture of emotions and feelings including some difficult bridges that I needed to cross. The most difficult of which was telling my adopted dad, the man who was and always will be my dad first and foremost. He fed me, clothed me, educated and loved me like any father would do and now I had to drop a bombshell on him. I knew this was going to be one of the hardest things I had ever had to do. I chose to see him on my own- there was no point in deliberating about it but the reaction I got astounded even me.

As I relayed the story from the initial email to the present day, my dad was overwhelmed with emotion to the point of actually shedding tears, something I had never experienced, at least in my conscious memory, but in some ways it humbled me. I learnt that both my adopted mother and father had always been aware of the fact that I was searching for my roots, and although they never actually said as much. To be perfectly honest, there was no real need for them to, they fully supported me and knew it was only a matter of time when the day would arrive when the search was complete. From the very beginning they had never concealed the fact that I was adopted to anyone who cared to inquire. There was some surprise and some initial resentment, but that was only to be expected given the period and what can only be described as narrow-minded attitudes at the time. None more than my mums' father whose initial response to our adoption was 'why are you bringing these little bastards into the family?' Albeit an accurate description in terms of us being born out of wedlock, as far as he was aware anyway, it was a tad harsh.

My adoptive parents were proud of the fact that they had the ability to provide love and care for children who had abandoned or given up by their natural parents. My dad was genuinely pleased for me and said as much, we hugged and spoke for a considerable time about the events of the past few days and weeks all the while reaffirming his support for my quest. He pointed out to me that had my mother still been alive, she too would have been intrigued and equally supportive. It was at this point I informed him of my intention to travel to Australia and New Zealand to meet my sisters and parents. His reaction to the news was simple and to the point. 'Andrew, I wouldn't expect you to do otherwise'. I left his house that day totally and utterly elated, knowing I had his full support and blessing. To this day I will be forever grateful for that, it had been a difficult day for me initially but my fears were unfounded, and to be perfectly truthful, somewhat of an over-reaction but perhaps understandably so.

So what about my twin brother, where was he in all of this and what were his feelings and his reaction to all of this? Well, I am absolutely certain he would have no misgivings about me explaining his position on this. From the very early days when my initial enquiries into our adoption started he made it abundantly clear that he had no interest in any of it. He was resolute that as far as he was concerned our adoptive parents, brothers and sisters were the only family he had. I was somewhat surprised at his reaction but had to respect the fact that he didn't share my thirst for knowledge and the need to know more about how we started out in life.

Over the years since my initial discovery, I had often tried to make him listen to what I had to say about what I had found out with regard to our true parentage. This usually resulted in a mixture of reactions, ranging from anger to condemnation of what I was doing. Most of this occurred in the early days and as I grew and matured I learned to be more understanding of his feelings about it all and respected his views. However, we were now at a crossroads. I now had more than just names of people and places on a piece of paper, I had spoken to these people including his natural mother and father, and surely he would want to share in my excitement? After all this was as much a part of him as it was me.

Initially though it was the usual nonplussed attitude that I came up against. I just couldn't seem to impress upon him the magnitude of the information I now had. However there was a spark of interest I noted when I mentioned the fact that our natural parents were both married, alive and both living in New Zealand. Slowly but surely he started to ask questions, until eventually there was no stopping him and he wanted to know everything, even from my initial findings all those years ago at a time when he had scorned my actions.

I have to say at this juncture though, and I am sure some may think with a somewhat selfish attitude, that I was not as forthcoming as I probably could have been, for example I had not mentioned that I was due to be meeting Jill and Ken in a matter of days. From my perspective though, this was the culmination of a long journey that he had not wanted to be a part of; I had considered it but put it out of my mind almost immediately. I had told him though that I had spoken to Clare on the phone and more than once and spoken about him, albeit briefly and not in detail as that was for him to do as and when he was prepared to do so if at all. I also told him that yes, I had spoken to our natural parents and that they would love to hear from him as well but that I was no way going to pressurise him into doing so.

It would have to be his decision; his reaction however was one I hadn't expected.

He wanted the phone number there and then, he couldn't seem to grasp the fact that you just couldn't ring someone up after forty years out of the blue even if they were your natural parents and when I refused point blank to give it to him, the age old resentment crept in and it was as if he felt that I was trying to prevent him from becoming drawn into something that what was rightfully his and something he should be allowed to deal with any way he pleased.

I have to say that at this point I bitterly regretted having made the decision to tell him all that I just had, I had this hopeless feeling and sensation of apprehension that it was all about to go horribly wrong and there wasn't anything I could do to prevent it happening. So I left not having given him any phone numbers but with the promise that I would let him have them as soon as I had paved the way for him, something he was somewhat aggrieved about, but as far as I was concerned was how it was going to be. In retrospect it was the right decision to make and he did eventually contact his natural parents both by mail and by phone, how his relationship panned out is however personal to him and not for me to document here. I was never privy to the conversations they had or the letters that were exchanged between them. I don't expect to be and I certainly wouldn't presume to be told either.

One of the nicest episodes that occurred as a result of my emails to the other side of the world, involved someone who had no family link. The lady in question is a quite wonderful person, Jill Marshall of Tourism Rotorua in New Zealand. I was desperate to find details of my natural parents adopted hometown and scoured the internet for any information I could find that would bring me closer to them. I came across a website for Tourism Rotorua, however after e-mailing them I was told that the images and photographs they had were only available on a commercial basis for companies wanting to promote the area. Undeterred I emailed Jill and told her my reasons for wanting some photographs, albeit briefly. The response was as follows and unequivocal.

We don't normally allow use of our Rotorua images in this way but what a wonderful thing to find your birth parents after forty years. So here is our treat for you. All the best and I hope that your visit here next year is everything you want it to be.

Attached to the e-mail were photographs of my natural parent's hometown, what a fantastic and unexpected response, it seemed only right that I should enlighten Jill more than I had already.

Thank you so much for your kind e-mail and the photos of my parent's hometown. I have been overwhelmed by my discovery, after all forty years is a long time. Just to give you some idea of the scale of my discovery, both my parents have lived in Rotorua since the 1970's having moved to and married in Auckland initially. They had to give my twin and I up for adoption in 1963 against all their wishes and had treasured a last photo and birth tags ever since. However that is all in the past now, I actually spoke to both my parents on the phone last night for the first time. An experience I will never forget, as an added bonus I now have gained two sisters and a brother, all who live in Australia. Suffice to say it has been an incredible time for me.

Once again thanks for your e-mail and the gift of the photos, it has just added to the immense feeling of happiness and euphoria that I have been experiencing of late.

The next e-mail from Jill left me positively tingling with anticipation and mixed emotions but also an element of excitement. You have to appreciate that all this was still all very new and exhilarating and to a degree it was almost like accepting a form of celebrity status. The euphoria and need to share it with everyone who wanted to know about it was almost irresistible.

Thanks for sharing your special story. When you do come out next year I would love to be able to tell the local newspaper about your discovery and meeting you if you were agreeable. Like most people, I love to hear good news when the world is so full of bad these days. Think about it and keep in touch. In the meantime enjoy your new family to the fullest.

I of course accepted by return email, after all why wouldn't anyone want to be in the local paper and achieve minor celebrity status albeit a world away from home. After all, wasn't it Andy Warhol who said 'In the future everyone will be famous for fifteen minutes'?

Damian and Tamara, two of my wonderful children, were to all intents and purposes oblivious to the impact this was having on their dad. Damian at the age of fifteen had an understanding of the adoption process and what it meant having been adopted and the possible reasons for the process to have been put in place. But to be fair to him, his mum and dad were with him, always had been and as far as he was concerned always would be. That said he was amazed by the revelations that he now had relatives in Australia and New Zealand and that dad now not only had brothers, sisters and a dad in the United Kingdom but also on the other side of the world as well. The whole thing (as you would expect) confused Tamara, as she was considerably younger, only six. She understood that she had her Nan (her mum's mother) and her Granddad (my adoptive dad) and all the associated aunts, uncles and cousins. However she also now had a new Nan and Granddad in New Zealand, an Aunt and Uncle in Perth, an Aunt and Uncle in Adelaide and an Uncle elsewhere in

Australia, but what she was not entirely clear about was where they had materialised from or why she had not heard of them up until now. To save any further confusion we left the further revelations of new cousins to a later date.

I did sit down and explain to Tamara about how some children are not able to be brought up and loved and cared for by their own mummies and daddies and that sometimes they have to go and live with other mummies and daddies who love and care for them just as much as their real mummies and daddies would have wanted to do. Although she was not entirely sure why this happened, she was more than happy in the knowledge that the children were safe and happy although sometimes they did miss their real mummy and daddy and that is why daddy had found his mummy and daddy and his brothers and sisters. As it stands now, both Damian and Tamara have gained so much by everything they have experienced both through my journey and me and by their own discoveries and experiences and I am in no doubt whatsoever that they have as much love and respect for their new family members as they do for the old.

Six

The Journey Begins

FINALLY, AFTER ALL THE planning and organising from arranging time off for Damian and Tamara from school, to planning the route and sorting out accommodation, the day had finally arrived. I had arranged for a local company to collect us and drive us to the airport and the Mercedes S Class duly arrived with the Chauffer as promised. The 3rd of April 2004, a very significant day in my life apart from the birth of my two children. This was to be the culmination of a journey that had started so many years before when I had seen what had appeared to be an inconsequential document in my dad's file. A document that bore my date of birth but a different name to the one I was known by, that name being Simon Lingwood. To this day I would not be able to tell you what the inside of Terminal Four at Heathrow is like or recall anything about the check-in. It seems curious now, but most of the initial part of the journey seems to have paled into irrelevance. As you can probably understand, despite all my best efforts, whilst my family eventually slept overnight heading towards Singapore, I struggled to close my eyes and drift off, my mind racing with the events and situations that lay ahead of us. Fear, doubt and excitement all rolled into one, what was I doing, what on earth was I hoping to achieve, dragging my family across to the other side of the world to stay with people we had never met. Would they like me? Let alone want me descending on them with my whole family in tow? Of course they would, we had talked about little else for over six months, but still there was an element of doubt, something was bound to go wrong, after all a month was a long time away from home in such a highly charged emotional situation such as this. We arrived in Singapore in the afternoon on the 4th April, stopping over for the night prior to flying down to Perth. Singapore was stunning, but my mind was elsewhere and vanished in a whirl of eating and sleeping amongst the extremely humid climate and singsong chatter of the locals. Bizarrely, the one thing about Singapore that I do recall is when we went for an early evening stroll and came across an open-air line dancing school, with a vast number of people all dressed as cowboys and cowgirls.

The day I was due to meet Clare for the first time dawned, I know we had breakfast prior to heading back to the airport but where, when and what, I know not. We boarded for the four-hour flight to Perth and having flown for thirteen hours the previous day, the four hours seemed to run away and before we knew it we were on the descent into Australia and my sister waiting on the other side of Customs. I kept being asked if I was okay and to be honest my heart was pounding.

Unlike my meeting with Jill and Ken in London, this time I knew what Clare and David looked like, due to the numerous photographs that had passed between us. But this did nothing though to allay the butterflies in my stomach, perhaps it was due to the location being unfamiliar territory so far from home and the anticipation of the meeting. I was more nervous this time round.

However, like Jill, the recognition was instantaneous but the oddest feeling was that this was perfectly natural and like coming home. All the anticipation and nervousness evaporated the instant I laid eyes on Clare. This was my sister and although we had never met, it seemed we had always known each other and that she was just meeting us after an extended holiday. It was an amazing and extraordinary experience and whilst walking across the car park I had a grin as wide as the ocean we had just crossed to get here. The week was a whirlwind of reminiscing, exchanging stories and catching up on over forty years worth of birthdays and Christmas, after all we both had missed out on 18th, 21st, 30th, and 40th birthdays, engagements, weddings, birth of my son and birth of my daughter; all pretty major events in most people's lives.

We talked about our childhoods and how we grew up, the schools we went to, our chosen career paths and the similarities in likes and dislikes. Whilst in Perth I also got to meet two other very important people. They were Clare, Jill and Stephen's brother James, and his wife Emma, who had both moved out to Australia that year. Back home in the United Kingdom was Louisa as well, along with Clare, Jill and Stephen's stepmother Carole. By now my family had grown beyond anything I could have imagined six months prior to this point.

However, something that was far more relevant and poignant was that whenever we went out, whether it was to the local Restaurant at Chapel Farm or to the local Wineries, I was always introduced as Clare's brother, not half brother, adopted brother or anything comparable but as her brother. That one word meant so much to me, it was a sign of absolute acceptance and was unconditional affection that only a sister and brother could have. Recognition of the fact that no matter what, no matter where we were, we both now had someone else we could call upon at anytime for any reason, even if it was just to talk about anything that happened along. What an extraordinary feeling, and one that will remain with me ad infinitum. For years I had brothers and sisters who were always there for me. But now I also had a sister who looked like me, thought like me and was of the same genetic structure as me, who to all intents and purposes felt like me and thought like me. As I have mentioned before, something that the majority of us take for granted, but for me, was the start of a whole new ball game. Life was good and getting better all the time, what struck me most was that here I was on the other side of the world with my family around me, revelling in the fact that I was experiencing the culmination of a voyage and yet I was completely at home. I experienced an overwhelming sense of belonging, which as the week went on, got stronger but in some ways became quite unsettling; after all, it was not as if when we eventually returned home that I would be able to just drop in because I was passing. Even now when I speak to Clare or David on the phone it leaves me with a measure of sadness. I miss them desperately and although it may seem strange to some, but watching or reading about Australia (in particular Perth where Claire and David live or Adelaide where Jill lives) does nothing to alleviate the pain and anguish.

Only recently in the UK there was a recruitment campaign by South Australia Police aimed at British Police Officers, so you can only imagine what I felt when one of the lads who I joined with as a Communications Operator (and who had later become a Police Officer) informed me he was transferring to Adelaide.

However, that said, you have to be realistic and somewhat philosophical about life. My chosen career was not one that would allow me to immigrate to Australia, and to even consider it would be self-centred. All of my life, my family and my home were in the UK and to consider dropping it all on a whim was not an option. That said, there is absolutely nothing wrong in having dreams and I don't think anyone would condemn me for having them under the circumstances.

Before we could catch our breath the week was over and it was off on the next leg of the journey to Adelaide to see Jill. This was in some respects more poignant, after all, when I had last met Jill she was on her own journey of discovery in the UK with Ken. We were now meeting again which, although was no doubt going to be incredibly exhilarating, was going to be tinged with sadness as the loss of Ken was still acutely felt by all, even Damian and Tamara were mindful of the situation. Ken, whilst in the UK, had given them Australian dollars to spend when they arrived in Adelaide and to this day I know they still have those coins which were given to them with genuine affection in the knowledge that we would all be together in Australia. It was tragic that this was not to be the case. Leaving Perth was harder than I had expected and it was only now that I realised that this trip was going to consist of an awful lot of breathtaking hello's and moving goodbyes, and that my emotions were in for a battering.

So it was goodbye Perth, hello Adelaide and into an emotional reunion with Jill. Tears flowed and feelings ran high as we all hugged each other, acknowledging the pain and loss we all felt and understood in our own but infinitely significant ways. One amazing surprise in Adelaide was meeting Jill's daughter Alison and her significant other, Travis. That would make Alison my niece I guess. How incredible, I now had a niece who was an adult. Back home all my nieces and nephews were under the age of four. But, even now looking back, I don't think we ever sat down and talked about how she felt about having another Uncle, but you have to understand, that from my perspective, I was just so relaxed and comfortable with the situation that it was never an issue. I never felt the need to question anything about the relationship between my newly discovered family and me.

We left the airport in convoy in two cars and headed for Gawler, located just north of Adelaide in the area known as the Barossa Region. We had decided to take a holiday home when we booked the trip, out of respect for Jill and her current circumstances. It had been recommended by Clare and David, who had stayed there when last visiting Jill.

It was out of this world and, in retrospect, it was a wise decision. Jill was in the throws of moving house so in limbo with regard to accommodation and the last thing she would have needed was me and my brood descending on her. Jill spent from early morning until late in the evening with us every day we were in Gawler. We explored the region and experienced the Australian Bush in its many different guises both at night and during the day. Once again I met people who were warm and accepting of both me and my family and who, as in Perth, were amazed by the story of how I found my sisters, brother and parents. There are photographs that were taken at the time and the one thing that stands out in all of them is how incredibly happy everyone is. They speak volumes about the situation and the circumstances that we found ourselves in and are a permanent reminder of a truly wonderful experience.

It was whilst we were in Adelaide one day that I became aware of some doubts about some of the validity of the information given to me about my parentage. It was at the same time as we were on the beach at Glenelg Jill and Damian were on the pier and Tamara was racing around on the sand. I had gone after her having called her numerous times to join us when Jill mentioned that my mannerism, disposition and demeanour were so like her father's and to that end there had been conversations between Clare and Jill since our arrival in Adelaide about the uncanny, but obvious resemblances they could see in relation to their father.

This, surprisingly enough, was not something that I had even considered and as far as I was concerned was purely coincidental and nothing else, given we didn't even have the same father. After all I knew who my father was and he was in New Zealand with my mother.

However alarm bells started to ring, after all both Jill and Clare knew their father far better than anyone else ever could... so what if there was an element of doubt that I should be considering? After some careful contemplation and more deliberation about the evidence in my possession, I dismissed any doubts that I may have had. After all, I had information given to me at my initial meeting with Social Services, which gave me the name of my father and mother.

Again, all too soon time in Adelaide ran out and the culmination of the trip was fast approaching when I would finally get to meet my natural parents. Leaving Australia was an odd experience as I felt I was leaving something very significant behind. I would be the first to admit that I am not an emotional kind of person but for once in my life I was moved to tears, my emotions were uncontrollable and I would swear to this day that if someone had approached me on that last day and said you don't have to go back to the UK, rightly or wrongly, I would be living in Australia now.

Seven

Welcome to New Zealand

'LADIES AND GENTLEMEN WE are now commencing our descent into Auckland', those words will stay with me forever. After all these years and numerous searches that had ended with negative results, I was finally only one day away from meeting my natural parents. We had one overnight stay in Auckland and would then travel south to Rotorua and into the arms of my waiting parents. It was all planned down to the last detail.

    The hire car company would collect us from the hotel and we would then drive south, so you can imagine my torment when the hire company didn't arrive at the time specified and two hours later we were still waiting for them. My nerves were in tatters but finally we were on our way, the RAV4 was loaded, my nerves were restored and the final leg of the journey lay ahead. I had no idea how long it was going to take and it had been agreed that I would ring my parents when we reached Rotorua for final directions. I should point out, that at my meeting with Social Services, I was advised that ideally the meeting should be on neutral territory, for example the hotel lobby where we were staying, and that I should initially meet them on my own before bringing the rest of the family into the reunion. I respected their views and the thought process behind the suggestions, but circumstances dictated that I would be meeting my parents at their house. Following on from conversations prior to the trip, their age and mobility were significant in the making of that decision as well as their insistence that we stayed with them and not in a hotel. But that wasn't a problem, as it had been agreed that I would be dropped off to allow me to meet them on my own as suggested, and the rest would come back after an agreed time of about an hour.

Before too long the road signs were counting down the miles to Rotorua and we finally arrived outside the Post Office at Nongataha just outside Rotorua and I stopped to make the call. I was completely calm whilst making the call, understandable really as I had spoken to them on numerous occasions on the phone already. The only peculiar aspect of the call was that there was no time difference to consider and that they were about ten minutes drive down the road, I think it was about now that I moved into unfamiliar territory and nagging doubts surfaced. I had no idea why, I just realised that something extraordinary was about to occur and that I was at the point of no return. All kinds of thoughts and feelings began to surface. Was my life about to undergo massive emotional upheaval? After all, I was about to meet my mother and father for the first time ever in my life.

Over forty years of separation finally narrowed down to a journey of mere minutes to their front door. So the final lap of the journey began. To this day I can picture the route from outside that Post Office if I shut my eyes I can retrace each and every mile, every turning the road took and buildings we passed. About halfway there I suddenly pulled over to the side of the road into a lay by, I had changed my mind about meeting them on my own. I wanted, no, needed, my family with me at the most crucial point of the whole experience, there was no way I could do this on my own, no matter what anyone else had advised me. There was absolutely no way I was going to walk that lonely path into a life changing experience.

Here I was on the other side of the world in a strange country with the only familiar part of my life sitting about two feet away from me, my family. My family supported me one hundred percent and promised me without any doubt that they would be there with me whatever my decision at the time. By this time my heart was racing and to say there were butterflies in my stomach would be an understatement. Finally, there was the long driveway up to the house. I had seen and pored over numerous pictures of the location, so it was instantly recognisable but still slightly unreal.

In order to park I had to drive past the house and the veranda, upon which sat two familiar people, familiar in that I had seen them in photographs. I parked up and stepped down from the RAV4 and walked towards these two people standing before me, mindful of the fact that despite my misgivings, my family were not following me. At this point you have to appreciate that I had read numerous accounts of what to expect in terms of an outpouring of emotion and almost unbearable feelings of longing and unequivocal love so I was prepared for anything that was to be thrown at me. I expected everything but I was to be in for a surprise because there was nothing, no tears, no breaking down and no incredible feelings of any sort, the kind you see on the television, which caught me completely off my guard. It was almost as if I had only been away for a couple of years and was returning home.

Hugging my mother and my father for that matter was like hugging my grandparents. I guess looking back on it now I was somewhat disappointed and it was far more of an anti-climax than I had been prepared for. Eventually the rest of the family joined us and there were more hugs and warm greetings but for me something was missing, I couldn't put my finger on it at all but something wasn't right. I shrugged it off and we all went into the house and the commencement of what was to be a very strange and enlightening couple of weeks.

The next few hours were spent, as you would expect, unpacking and talking. We had of course spoken at length over the phone but now we were face to face and yet still the conversation mainly centred around the here and now as opposed, as you would expect, the past. I had questions about what had happened back in 1963, why had I been adopted? Why couldn't they have kept me? Why if they were still together now hadn't they wanted to keep me etc? Oh, so many more questions but none that I asked. I was still feeling slightly uncomfortable without knowing why and I had my family to think of as well.

We had been away from home now for over three weeks and certainly for Tamara it was starting to become a bit much and she was starting to miss some of the routine of her home life, in particular her Nan and her friends at school, to that end she wanted her dad to comfort her and sit with her whilst she drifted off to sleep that first night in a strange house far away from home.

My mother, strangely, was not so understanding and insisted I left her alone and come and talk to them, after all, we were only in the other room and this was our first night together, plus they had something important to tell me. I persisted with Tamara who eventually fell asleep and joined the rest of the family.

Great excitement ensued, whilst we had been in Australia my mother had been busy and had arranged a photo shoot and interview with the local press, something we had talked about following on from the email conversations between me and Jill Marshall in Rotorua. However, the press day had been arranged for 8 o'clock the next morning, something which, to be honest, horrified me totally. Although I fully acknowledge that the idea of a story and photograph for the local paper was partly engineered by me, I had expected at least some kind of settling in period before any outside involvement, supposing it ended up going horribly wrong, and we didn't get on or worse?

Still there was nothing I could do about it now, it was already late evening and it had been a long day already. I had a strange sense of foreboding but put that down to a mixture of emotions and the circumstances. I also learnt further that my mother and father had changed their will and that I was to be a beneficiary of land on which I could, if

I chose, build a house. One question they did ask was whether or not I was going to revert back to the surname I was given at birth, not only this but they still insisted on calling me Simon, and not Andy, which was the source of some amusement to Tamara and Damian.

I pointed out that I had been Andy for forty years and was not considering changing my name to anything else. After all, it was the name I was christened with and the name everybody knew me by and so we retired with the promise of another day and yet more revelations ahead.

A new day dawned and right on cue the press arrived at the allotted time, one reporter and one photographer. I had all my family gathered together for a family photograph but was somewhat surprised when my mother wanted one of just me, her and my father. I appreciated that it was a huge thing for them being re-united with their son again after so long so the picture was duly taken and the details of our discovery were passed on to the reporter from The Daily

Post... all this before breakfast! Apparently it would be in the next edition which was the subsequent day.

In the meantime, mindful of the fact that my parents were of a certain age and not used to having company, in particular young children, I decided we would head off into Rotorua for some local sightseeing and give them some time to recover from the initial shock. We spent a very pleasant day wandering round the Rotorua area soaking up the sun and the culture of New Zealand and planning the next couple of weeks, all the places we would visit and things we would do whilst in the area. Evening again, and we made our way back 'home' for dinner with my parents, stopping on the way to buy my father a bottle of malt whisky and my mother some wine. This small gesture may not seem much to most, but I had never bought my mother and father anything before. Again, that evening, the conversation turned to my plans for the future and our move to New Zealand. This was something that had been mentioned in our many conversations and I would be the first to admit that, whilst back home in Britain, the idea of emigrating to New Zealand had its attractions - not least of all cheap housing, the possibility of a career doing what I wanted to do and a near perfect climate and safe environment for the kids to grow up in.

However, now I was there, realisation kicked in. My mother and father were so enthusiastic about it all, which even now I wonder about. I was, at this point, starting to feel somewhat uncomfortable. They still hadn't asked me about my childhood, coming to terms with the realisation that I had been adopted and how it was for me growing up, about my mum and dad, brothers and sisters and the usual kind of things you would expect a mother and father to ask their son.

That said, I was now painfully aware of how hard their life had been up until they moved out to New Zealand, how perfect their relationship had been since they met all those years ago.

But what about their other children who had also been abandoned on both sides of the family? I knew about Jill, Claire and Stephen, but why had it taken so long for my mother to want to trace her first born and subsequent children? After all, following the breakdown of her marriage, it taken until the 1980's for her to make contact again?

What about my father's side of the story? This is somewhat hazy, but as far as I understood there were at least one boy and two girls, and therefore I now had additional step siblings to add to my family tree. However, my father was not keen to talk about them, other than to point out that two of them didn't speak to him anyway and that at least one of them had experienced a somewhat colourful lifestyle.

So many questions and very few answers and so another day dawned and the arrival of copies of the local newspaper. Sure enough, on the front page for the entire world to see was a photograph of me and my long lost parents. The article was titled 'Tears of Joy at Reunion' but I will let that go as poetic licence, because there were certainly no tears at the first meeting. The rest of the article made for interesting reading as well, most of it was completely factual but all of a sudden we were no longer just thinking of moving to New Zealand. My family and I were moving to New Zealand and building a house on land at the front of my parents' house and looking for a job. Now I don't deny that we had mentioned it and discussed the remote possibility that it could happen, but according to the article I was actively planning to do just that. I had family back home, a career and a life that I was not just about to dismiss overnight and move to other side of the world on a whim. I wasn't incensed by the article, just somewhat surprised by it, though I should have learnt by now that on occasion if you fuel the fire you should expect to get burnt at some point.

We had planned a trip that day to find a beach for Tamara but I also felt the need to get away and have some space. I don't know what it was but I was starting to feel uncomfortable with the whole scenario and yet something kept me hanging on. We drove off with some vague directions about how to get to beach and ended up on the coast, the whole place was deserted but we spent a pleasant enough day exploring the coast from Maketu down to Whakatane whilst discussing what was happening and how we all felt about it all. Something that was becoming all too apparent was that my parents, whether it was intentional or not, were managing to isolate Tamara and her mum. Tamara, being only 6, was unlikely to have been aware of it but her mum was only too well aware and was feeling understandably very uneasy about it. Perhaps they foresaw and felt something I couldn't even anticipate with my former wife, but my daughter surely not? Damian, on the other hand, couldn't put a foot wrong and they were ensuring that he knew as much, which to be fair made it very awkward for him.

This was to become more apparent with a later incident; however we now had to head for home.

Time was suddenly against us, being on the other side of the world meant that night was drawing in earlier than we had anticipated, however we got to see the sun going down over the lake at Rotoiti It was magnificent in it's splendour and as we were stopped, I took the opportunity to ring my mother and father to let them know we would be a little late home. I was reassured that it was no problem at all, dinner was on but it could be turned down pending our arrival. So one final run around the beach and in and out of the climbing frame and we set off for dinner and an evening of further fact finding. We got back to Rotorua but went a different way around the lake and ended up missing a turning; after all, we were in a strange country, it was dark and the roads were not well signed. We eventually got back an hour later than anticipated and tumbled through the door for dinner. What met us stunned us into complete and utter silence. No dinner and no parents, they had taken themselves and the dog off to bed. Now bear mind it was still only half past seven at night and we were not that late. I was aghast, what on earth did they think they were doing? Not only had they not considered that perhaps something had happened to us, after all we were in a strange country, but they had left no food out or provision for any food and I had two hungry children to feed. I was absolutely incensed to the point that I even considered packing to leave. I didn't know what to say; after all I had bought my family all the way out there and here was I feeling like a naughty schoolboy. I was 41 for goodness sake but was being made to feel about 12. We managed to sort our own dinner out that night and after Damian and Tamara had gone to bed I sat and considered the day's events and what we should do and not once was there any movement from my parent's room. I think I had decided that enough was enough by the time we went to bed and the contingency plan I had made was about to come into play. Little did I know it but things were not going to get much better.

We got up the next day to a breakfast of silence and an extremely uncomfortable atmosphere. Thank God for my children, who were oblivious to what was going on, although Damian was probably more aware due to his age. My mother chose not to leave the bedroom for the early part of the morning and my father retreated to his favourite place in the house, namely the dining table overlooking the veranda where he silently rolled cigarette after cigarette. The atmosphere was horrendous, despite trying to make conversation, I even apologised for any offence I may have caused due to us being late home though, to be perfectly frank, I am not sure why I even tried. Finally, I took the bull by the horns and informed my father we were heading into town. Rotorua was fast becoming a favourite place to be.

On a lighter note we had found this excellent family restaurant which went quite aptly by the name of 'Fat Dog Café and Restaurant' located at 1161 Arawa Street, Rotorua. Just down the street from Rotorua's main information centre and directly opposite the Court House. I would heartily recommend a visit if ever you are in Rotorua, their pancakes are to die for. Today though was another significant day for me as I was going to meet Jill Marshall from Tourism Rotorua, the very kind lady who had sent me photographs of my parent's hometown all those months ago. We all trooped up the staircase to the top floor of the Tourism Building only to be told that Jill was at lunch. No matter, we could wait for her. In fact, when they realised who I was, we were ushered into the conference room where a meeting had been in progress and plied with cakes and coffee and urged to tell my story. Imagine the scene if you will, a group of people who I had never met, including Jill, who by now had arrived back, all sitting around a table in a building on the other side of the world hanging on my every word as I retold my story from August 2003 to the present day. Then being bombarded with questions which were all answered without reservation or hesitation about my childhood and where I grew up, my family, what brothers and sisters did I have how my dad felt about it all. They asked all about my sisters and brother in Australia, where were they living and what was their reaction to it all.

It's funny really but on reflection that wonderful group of people asked me more questions about my family at home and in Australia and about my childhood than my parents did. I will be forever grateful for that, they restored my faith in people and the reason why I was in New Zealand. It was with a heavy heart, however, that we returned to my parent's house following another visit to Fat Dog's for ice cream and coffee. Yes, even after having cleared Tourism Rotorua out of cakes and pastries.

My mother had finally decided to venture out of the bedroom and again I offered my apologies for our apparent lateness the previous evening. There, unsurprisingly, was no reciprocation for their behaviour though, but some semblance of tranquillity had returned and at least they were talking to us again. I went for a walk around the 'promised land' that I had been told I could build our house on when we moved to New Zealand. The location itself is idyllic with only the sound of deer and other indigenous wildlife to disturb you. Passing vehicles are minimal and it would be naive of me to say that it would not be a fantastic place to build a house. However, then take into consideration the distance to town, and the distance you would have to drive to the nearest village shop, and you realise that tranquillity and isolation go hand in hand and, thinking about it, realistically the possible reason why my parents were like they were was probably due to having spent so many years in isolation. All of a sudden they had a son, daughter in-law and two grandchildren descend on them and they just couldn't cope with it.

This however, was no excuse for what happened that evening, dinner passed off quite amicably, albeit somewhat strained in terms of conversation. My father by now said very little anyway. Damian had finished his dinner and had taken his plate out to the kitchen with my mother in tow, shortly afterwards I became aware of raised voices and went to investigate. I found my mother offering Damian a large tin of chocolate bars and various sweets, not usually a problem except that my mother had said that it was just for him and not Tamara as she didn't deserve any. Damian, as he always is, was protective of his sister and standing his ground pointing out that if Tamara wasn't having any then neither was he. My mother was insisting he take some and not tell her, but still he refused and by now he was getting quite agitated. I pointed out to her that she couldn't do what she was doing with my children, they were both equal and should be treated the same. Imagine my reaction however when my mother said that Tamara was spoilt and was obviously always the centre of attention where as Damian was always left out of things. Damian was mortified by these revelations and pointed out in no uncertain terms that his grandmother was wrong on all counts.

Once again fuming at the crass stupidity of my mother's actions, we went back to the lounge with chocolate in hand for both Damian and Tamara, but quite obviously against my mother's wishes. What happened next is beyond belief even to this day. Tamara was sat with me enjoying her hard won chocolate, although she had no idea what had occurred prior to this, when my mother suddenly appeared with a small figurine of the Madonna and sat on a chair in front of Tamara. She asked her if she would like the little statue. Tamara of course, full of enthusiasm, said yes she would, after all it was a present from her Nan. To my horror and obvious dismay my mother then insisted that Tamara kiss the Madonna and promise to be a good girl from now on and that if she did as Nan had asked then she could have the little statue for herself. My father even joined in with her and sat there encouraging this ridiculous and almost nauseating setting. Tamara, thankfully, has no recollection of any of the events of that evening. But it was more or less the final straw and that night I packed our bags. I needed to put some distance between us and my parents and as soon as possible.

The following morning I finally got to speak to my father somewhere other than at the dining table. I explained our feelings and how I felt that we all needed to give each other some space as things had quite obviously not panned out as we had all hoped. He was quite reticent about it all and more or less agreed that it was probably for the best. He quite rightly, from his perspective, pointed out that the last few days had not been easy for my mother, but in my opinion this did not excuse or justify her behaviour or how she had treated both my children. However, being ever the diplomat, I refrained from making any comment and passing judgement on the situation. Instead I explained what our plans were for the next few days. We had decided to take advantage of the situation and travel further a field and discover more of their adopted country. We had picked up a map and a book listing hotels and motels to stay at whilst we had been in Rotorua the previous day. I told my father that whatever happened we would be back in time for my birthday on the 29th of April. I was only too well aware that as it was to be the first birthday I had ever spent with my parents and they had arranged to go out for the evening and had planned to make it a special night with various people invited.

So the RAV4 was loaded up again, although we had decided to leave a couple of bags behind that we didn't need for the trip and off we went. As we drove up the drive the tension and the mood lifted and you could almost feel the sense of relief. We headed north and made for Mount

Maunganui where we spent three fabulous days just messing about on the beach by day or climbing the volcano and just spending time together as a family, our accommodation was superb and overlooked the beach and having re-established our self esteem as a family we set off across country to experience some of the wonders of New Zealand

My birth parents, Sally and Ted 2004

Eight

The Final Outcome

AS MENTIONED PREVIOUSLY, THE intention was always to return to my parent's house in Rotorua for my birthday and that was one engagement I proposed to keep. By now the weather was inclement in New Zealand and at times we could have been back home in the United Kingdom the weather was that atrocious. It almost suited the mood of the time and place we had now reached; we had in some ways quite sadly reached a point in our trip where regret was becoming the word of the day. Regret that we had decided to spend two weeks in New Zealand and not more time in Australia or extended our planned stay in our next stopover, Los Angeles. We had booked ourselves into a motel overlooking Lake Rotorua a fantastic place right on the beach which would have been absolutely perfect had it not been for the persistent drizzle and overcast skies. It was the 29th of April and my 41st birthday I had received cards over breakfast from my family and a card I had carried with me all the way from the United Kingdom from a work colleague. Small tokens but so very much appreciated so far away from home. Damian was not well, so whilst Tamara and I headed off to my parents, his mum decided she would stay and look after him, although deep down she just knew she could not face my parents again, something I fully appreciated and understood.

So it was with a heavy heart and a sense of foreboding that Tamara and I left them behind, the first time in the whole trip that we had been apart. Tamara chattered away in the passenger seat about how she was looking forward to seeing Nanny and Granddad again, as well as their small Jack Russell 'Tara'. God bless the innocence of small children, I know one day she will be old enough to read and understand what actually happened in New Zealand but what she should know is that she played a big part in keeping my feet on the ground and keeping me from making decisions and saying things that I might have regretted. The atmosphere on arrival was thick enough to cut with a knife and the mood was as gloomy as the weather outside. From the outset it was destined to be a difficult visit, my birthday card was retrieved from the bin and thrust at me with the comment 'we had thrown this out but you may as well have it as you're here now'. It transpired that whatever plans they had made for the day had been cancelled, it would seem not long after we left either. I pointed out that it was their prerogative to have done so and I certainly would not presume otherwise. The conversation was bitter and condescending at best. All the talk of us moving out to New Zealand and building a house on the land now drenched in drizzle and shrouded in mist, just outside the window, had now evaporated.

Indeed I was now being told that circumstances had changed and that the land and house were now going to the state in order to allow them some extra income whilst they were still alive. A scheme I wholeheartedly agreed with and condoned fully. I suspect they thought I might have contested their decision but I wanted nothing from them then and never had. I pointed out to them that at their time of life then they should be doing everything to make themselves comfortable and if that was one way of releasing some capital then they shouldn't hesitate in going ahead and signing the relevant documentation. I'd heard enough and I just wanted out of there, I gathered up our belongings that had been left behind prior to our sojourn across country, noting that certain personal items I had given them on our arrival had mysteriously been returned. So we left, Tamara still chatting away, oblivious to the tension and the situation and headed back to the rest of the family back at the motel by the rain soaked lake. Damian was no better and so the rest of the day was spent packing and keeping Tamara amused. I spent my 41st birthday surrounded by my immediate family which was quite right and proper and, for my birthday dinner, I had a couple of glasses of wine with a delicious cheese sandwich. A stark contrast to the celebration I was told I would be having in a popular restaurant with my mother and father and friends from Rotorua. The next day dawned with the return of the sun, not that we needed the sun to lift our spirits; we were on our way home, last stop Los Angeles for three days rest and recuperation. However there was one last thing to do before leaving New Zealand. I was prepared to give my parents one last chance to redeem themselves and we were going to descend on them one last time prior to heading north for

Auckland and the airport. I shouldn't have been surprised really, nothing had changed, and the reception was almost frosty. I was deeply saddened now by all the events that had occurred since arriving in New Zealand in so many ways I had prepared myself for any and every eventuality but that doesn't make it any easier to bear. I felt betrayed I guess, after all the warmth that had had seemed so evident in the numerous phone calls I had made prior to the trip, only to have found the complete opposite on our arrival. I was at a loss to understand why my family had been subjected to the treatment they had received.

No-one should be made to feel unwelcome anywhere, particularly so far away from home that kind of behaviour is unforgivable from anyone and yet there was still the nagging doubt at the back of my mind. Something just didn't seem right, something I had felt from day one but just couldn't put my finger on and it was something that would remain a mystery for sometime to come yet.

So we left, my enduring memory of our departure was the absence of my mother as we drove away and of my father standing on the veranda neither smiling or waving but just stood there, a solitary figure gazing across the field that was not so long ago destined to have a house built on it; a house which would become home to his son and his family. Something that, no matter what, was never going to happen in his lifetime or mine come to that.

The journey north passed quickly, stopping only once for refreshments, we were on a mission to leave New Zealand as soon as we possibly could. The hire car was dumped unceremoniously at the hire centre where only two weeks before I had been on a massive high having arrived in the very country my parents lived in and whom I was only hours away from meeting for the first time.

What a contrast now, it felt as though a whole lifetime had passed. I was almost urging the taxi on to the airport. A ten-hour flight to Los Angeles lay ahead, but that wasn't going to be a problem as far as we were concerned, we just wanted to be on the plane. But then at the airport (and it seemed just to add insult to injury) we discovered we had to pay to leave the country. Okay it was airport tax, but if it wasn't paid we would be delayed in leaving and so many forms to fill in as well. But at last we boarded and were away. I still had a twinge of sadness at what had come to pass on my first, and possibly last, visit to New Zealand. I settled back into my seat and tried to sleep, after all we were crossing another time zone and despite this being a night flight we would be landing in Los Angeles on the same day and two hours before the time we had taken off from New Zealand. How bizarre was that going to feel?

Nine

The Inevitable Fallout

LOS ANGELES, CITY OF 'The Angels', city of hopes and dreams for young and not so young aspiring actors and actresses pop stars and wannabees. Never having been a fan of America I was pleasantly surprised by what I found. The hotel was excellent, Hotel Marina Del Ray, which lay but a short walk from the world famous Venice Beach and a bit further along Santa Monica Beach, places instantly recognisable even by my children, and so many places to eat. It was the perfect antidote to the New Zealand experience. On the second day, having spent a fantastic time on the boardwalk of Venice Beach experiencing the sights and sounds of Muscle Beach, and the vast array of stalls, shops and café's, watching the locals shooting hoops on the basketball courts and just generally soaking up the atmosphere of scenes we had seen countless times on the television, I decided to check my emails courtesy of the hotel's internet access computer in the lobby. Something I had not done whilst in New Zealand, mainly because I never came across anywhere where access was readily available. Amongst all the inevitable junk emails there was a short email from my parents, it read as follows;

Well we trust that you feel proud of yourself. Was this a way of getting your own back after all these years because we had to have you adopted through no reason of our own? We said that Dad would have liked a short time alone with you but your reaction was that time with your family meant more. Surely sixty minutes would have not gone amiss? After all you have a lifetime with your family. To say we are heartbroken is putting it mildly. You built up our hopes and dreams of life together and we had planned so many things for us.

Well, you can imagine my reaction; I was completely and utterly stunned by the content. But what I had thought in New Zealand was borne out by an email that had been exchanged between my parents and Jill on the 27th April, two days prior to my return visit to my parents home you will recall, Jill had sent them an email as she was concerned that my visit had not gone as planned having spoken to us on the phone whilst we were staying on Lake Taupo in New Zealand. She had pointed out quite diplomatically that it was perhaps due to us all staying at their house, which was quite restrictive with regard to space but perhaps all was not lost as we were going to be returning on the 29th as planned. However their response to Jill left me with no doubt that I was correct in how they felt about my family; the rot was setting in as you will see;

We suspected that there was something wrong within a couple of days it is a pity but what can we do? We suspect that the problem lies with the female part of the family. What can we say, but we are heartbroken. All our plans and hopes seemed to have gone by the board. What more can we say?

They quite obviously felt that the blame if it was to be laid anywhere was firmly at the feet of my former wife and my daughter. I, as you can imagine, was incensed. At no time had they intimated that they had felt something was wrong, their only response to any issues was to lock themselves away in their bedroom along with the dog just as they had done on our second day with them. However, I was not about to let this ruin the last three days of our adventure to the antipodes. California was fantastic, but we were desperate now to get home and some familiar sights and sounds. So it was with mounting excitement that we boarded our seventh and final plane and headed for home. The final flight was as uneventful as the previous six had been, the only difference being that the destination was one that would hold no surprises for us just familiarity and home comforts and no doubt find us ankle-deep in mail and I was certain that all our family back home would be anxious to hear about all our adventures and the outcome of our various visits too. Of course it wasn't long before we had all settled back into our usual routines of school and work but I still had that last email from my parents nagging me to respond. I had of course spoken to both Clare and Jill since arriving back in the UK but still I was unsure how to respond if at all. However it wasn't until I came across an email that had been sent to my twin brother, Alistair that I decided it would be wrong of me not to respond in some way. The email to my brother was even more shocking than the one that had been sent to me and left me infuriated.

Again this had been sent on the 27th April two days before I was due back in Rotorua it read as follows;

Things have not turned out as we had hoped, needless to say your mum is heartbroken, and we have cancelled all the parties and barbecues that we had planned. I blame the females but there it is, but always remember that our home will always be open to you. We both hope that you will come and see us in the near future, perhaps you were right about Simon, and I think the word is hag ridden. At the moment I am trying to comfort your mum, but all the mardy about love and that is making it an uphill struggle, needless to say heritages have all gone by the board. I don't need to say that we still love you; it is an enormous pity that we can no longer say the same about Simon.

Just about summed everything up I think, I was again completely and utterly stunned, what a poisonous and vindictive email, not only that but they had sent it to my own brother, did they really think that he wouldn't have brought it to my attention? Of course he did, along with the fact that they had sent him a letter containing two cards that they had decided to send to him rather than entrust them to me. The phrase's 'perhaps you were right about Simon' and 'hag ridden' of course raised questions about what Alistair had said to provoke such comments, however I am not that naive that I don't think something had been said in conversation between the three of them about my marriage and my family and how others might perceive it. But I also believe that my parents were capable of misconstruing anything said to them as they saw fit. So it was that, eight days after arriving back in the UK, I penned my response to my parents, I was diplomatic but forthright in my riposte;

Well, that was something I didn't expect. Yes I am proud of myself and what I have achieved with my life. I have a wonderful family and two equally wonderful children who I would die for tomorrow if I had to. They have and always will come first. I will never let anyone come between them and I will never let anyone hurt them in any shape or form, be it physically or verbally. They are THE most important thing in my life and always will be. Some people would call that commendable, after all it's what being a family and having children is all about is it not?

As for suggesting that I was 'getting back at you' for what happened forty years ago. Do you really honestly believe that I would pay out a small fortune and travel to the other side of the world in order to get back at someone? I set out on my voyage of discovery with the best intentions in the world and that was to meet my mother and father. It has taken me twenty years to be able to make that trip and despite everything I am so pleased that I have at last achieved what I set out to do. The fact that you could not accept my family for the people they are is no-one else's fault but your own. Be under no illusion that my adopted family and in particular my dad love all my family to bits. They never have and never would try and change them in any way.

Tamara has an awful lot of energy and is on the go from morning until night, she is no more spoilt than Damian and is certainly not the centre of attention, but being a six year old she gets the attention from her parents that any normal parent would give a six year old. The tragedy of all this is that no matter how you treated her, in particular with regard to the Virgin Mother episode which incidentally left all of us absolutely appalled, Tamara still calls you her Nanny and Granddad in New Zealand, for that alone you should be eternally grateful.

By the way I saw Alistair (Ian) on Wednesday; the same day you left him a message on his answer phone asking him to ring you back. I have also seen the letter you sent him. I take it you didn't trust me to bring two cards back from yourselves for fear of them being 'mislaid'. I have to say that for a mother and father who profess to have had so much love for the sons you lost, you didn't take long to change your mind about me. I guess you just could not accept that I had a family and life in the UK and that the childhood I had was not far off perfect. Not that you ever got around to asking me about it or about my brothers, sisters or the man I call dad or the wonderful lady who was my mum. To them I will be forever grateful.

Make of this what you will, just be mindful of the fact that I did all the running in this voyage of discovery. I was the one who phoned every week to talk to you and made the plans to come out and see you and I did it all with genuine love and absolute honesty. It was you who decided that certain members of my family were 'distractions' and stopped us talking. Nothing could be further from the truth. Those members of my family were made to feel uncomfortable and unwanted from more or less day one and trust me I know what you truly think of 'the females' and I would not and could not allow them to feel that way so far away from home. You never appreciated that Tamara was only six, a long way from home, from her friends, family and the home comforts that make a child comfortable in their environment. You excluded her and yet you had the audacity to heap loads of love and attention on her brother whilst she was in the same room. That was nothing short of outrageous; you treated my family whilst we were in your care abysmally.

I leave you with those thoughts and perhaps you may see some reason in them. If you don't then there is something very selfish about the way you look at life. I learnt an awful lot from my time in New Zealand. I can only hope that you learnt from the experience as well.

Me (darker hair) and my twin brother Alistair

Ten

More Revelations

UNDER NORMAL CIRCUMSTANCES YOU would think that would be the end of the story and for a while it could have been had it not been for nagging doubts brought about by observations made by my newfound family in Australia and the situation that developed in New Zealand. After all both Clare and Jill had remarked about how similar I was with regard to certain characteristics to their father Ray. Surely biologically this would be impossible as Ted was my father... or was he? Those alarm bells started to reverberate incessantly in my head, could it be one of the reasons Sally and Ted had reacted the way they had when they saw me for the first time in forty years. Had they seen the same things that perhaps Clare and Jill had? Just suppose Ray was indeed my father and not Ted, after all my birth certificate named Ray as my father not Ted. Had Sally and Ted seen more of Ray in me and it had caused them more than a modicum of consternation? After all, the circumstances surrounding my conception, birth and subsequent adoption were still cloudy and had never really been explained and the details I had been given certainly didn't ring true with me. I had accepted what I had been told, what reason would I have to doubt the validity of the information given to me. At the time I had no one to confirm otherwise, but now I had discovered all these people who I could converse with and share views and theories with. Of course you could always argue that surely we had exchanged photographs and would be able to instantly see any similarities and of course you're absolutely right, but photographs can be interpreted in any way you desire and in some ways it is easy to see what you want to see, as opposed to what you can actually see. However, when you are face to face with people and living in each other's pockets for a period of time, other attributes and physical similarities far outweigh any previous thoughts one may have had.

I had a need to try and bottom this out and first stop was Dad, after all he would have been privy to information and details surrounding my pre-adoption, so perhaps he could shed some light on the current predicament I now found myself in. I was staggered by my dad's reaction; he wasn't at all surprised by my revelations. In fact, he even pointed out that when he and mum had adopted me, both of them had been told that Ray was indeed my father. He had always been aware of this and was in his words surprised that it could have been otherwise, which was why he had been astounded by the news back in 2003 when I had told him that I had discovered my mother and father both married and living together in New Zealand.

One therefore may question his motives with regard to not letting me know his thoughts before I travelled to the other side of the world. However, from his perspective and rightly so, I feel here was his son in front of him, absolutely ecstatic about having made all these discoveries, how on earth and why would he want to shatter the hopes and dreams before I had made the journey? There is always a chance that over time documented facts could be misconstrued or even 'adjusted' at the time to suit to the situation. In the 1960's extra marital pregnancies were to be frowned upon and were not acceptable so for the sake of decency and to maintain modesty and values perhaps administrative procedures were 'adjustable'. Second stop was Social Services and Jane who when I retold my story was somewhat amazed and pointed out that the facts she had to hand in what few details she had certainly told a different story about my parentage and again cast yet further doubt on the truth. Jane also revealed that the details they had and indeed the same details I had been given all those years ago in 1991 were all that they had available to them. However it now transpired there was an agency in London who had more documentation surrounding my adoption and that perhaps we should apply and have them released to look at. Jane only had to make the suggestion once and I signed over my authority for her to apply for the paperwork to be sent. What was I about to discover now, if anything after all I had been through, could this be the final piece in the jigsaw that would confirm or refute everything I had already discovered? Only time would tell and I had eight weeks to wait, possibly longer

A further revelation came about when Jill came over for a second visit in the spring of 2005. I travelled with her to just outside Southampton where she had arranged to stay with one of her aunts and uncles. I was fully aware of their existence and had always had in the back of my mind that I should meet them at some point and as it happens they were as keen to meet me as I was them. However it was with some trepidation that we finally turned into the close where they lived, having got lost numerous times on the way there. Once again I was to be dumbfounded on meeting Auntie Joan and Uncle Ken. Letting Jill lead the way, I held back slightly, after all this was Jill's moment, meeting her Aunt and Uncle for the first time since she tragically lost her husband Ken back in 2003. Of course they had spoken numerous times in the intervening period but this was the first time they had physically met since then. On crossing the threshold and walking into the lounge I was astounded to hear both Joan and Ken exclaim 'Oh my God' and 'He is just so like him no doubt about it'.

By him, they were referring to Ray, Clare, Jill and Stephens father and not as you would think Ted. There is no-one more qualified or able to make that observation, after all both had known Ray back in the 1960's, not only that, but Ken is Ray's brother. They had no doubt whatsoever as to whom my father was. The journey home later was one that consisted of a mixture of emotions. In a way it was the culmination of a long journey, on the one hand I had achieved everything I had set out to do but on the other I was no further forward. On leaving Auntie Joan and Ken I promised to return and bring my children with me but to date that has yet to happen. I am in no doubt that a return visit will happen though but I needed to take some time out. I had reached a point where I was becoming burnt out as well as overloaded with information, and felt that I needed to back pedal for a while whilst I regrouped and re-evaluated where I was with my life.

Clare, Jill and Dad had all had their own views on the subject of my true parentage, but had all kept their opinions to themselves and for that I am grateful. They were absolutely right to not say anything and as Clare said it was my journey and it was only correct and proper that I should find out and make my own mind up about what I uncovered during my passage. However I was now in a quandary. I knew full well that if I even tried to ask my mother and father for the truth I would be completely stonewalled.

However, what will always stick in my mind is how little Ted had said in the later stages of our visit and how he seemed to become more and more reticent. I had assumed that it was because of the atmosphere and how things had developed, but now I wasn't so sure. I can still remember the lone figure standing on the deck at the front of the house in New Zealand, watching us in the distance as we turned out of the drive and headed for Auckland on our last day, just standing and watching, no wave, nothing.

Was it pensive reflection on past events or was he thinking of someone else long since passed away who might have been my rightful father? I may never know now and it is something that will be taken to the grave unless someone can categorically stand up and claim paternal rights with absolute and unquestionable proof. There are ways and means, both scientific and non-scientific, of confirming either way, the non-scientific way amounts to more or less what I have stated above about eligibility being confirmed by word of mouth. Scientific of course would mean the ultimate paternity test by way of DNA testing, that however is not an avenue I intend to pursue. On the other hand I am now in possession of documents and letters that to my mind could prove my parentage unequivocally. Extracts from those documents all point to Ray being my birth father the most significant is as follows;

Your Birth Mother was:

Audrey May Lingwood (Sally)

Your Birth Father was:

Audrey's husband, Raymond Lingwood

You were born on the 29th April 1963 at Crawley Hospital, You were born by normal delivery; you weighed 6lbs and 6 oz's and were named Simon Lingwood. After leaving hospital you were placed in the care of a foster mother in Crawley. You stayed there longer than usual because you contracted chicken pox and could not be placed with adopters while infectious. This meant that you became very attached to the foster carers and their family, who wanted to keep you themselves. This however was not felt to be a good idea as they lived close to your birth parents.

Your birth father gave consent to your adoption as he could see no possibility of being able to look after all the five children. Audrey (Sally) was living in digs and could not provide for the babies. Both Ray and Audrey (Sally) were anxious that you should have a secure and stable childhood and not be moved from place to place.

You were brought to the NCAA Knightsbridge office on the 14th August 1963 and handed on the same day into the care of Mr. & Mrs. Angus. You were adopted by them on the 12th March 1964

On the application for adoption form, again under the heading of birth father, the name Raymond Lingwood and not Ted Harman appears, and both Audrey and Ray signed the form giving up all parental rights and the right to reclaim their infant at anytime.

Even more significant is a letter from Audrey (Sally) in 1996 to a Miss Christine West of The Family Placement Service whereby she states 'I remarried in Auckland New Zealand in 1974 and my husband is fully aware of the twins' existence' Even now still no mention of Ted being my birth father just a statement that he was 'fully aware of my existence.'

From my point of view, and indeed many others mentioned in the book, at this stage there was no doubt in our minds as to who my true father actually could be. However, as is usually the case in my life, nothing is that straight forward. Just recently I showed Michaela a photograph of Ted in full naval uniform when he was in his late teens. Bear in mind she had never seen any photographs up to this point and I didn't enlighten her as to who it was in the photograph in anyway, shape or form but her reaction was unequivocal. She saw me as I would have looked at the same age. Indeed, she actually thought it was a photograph of me in my uniform and was somewhat stunned to realise that in fact it was someone else entirely.

Likewise when I showed her a picture of Ted taken in New Zealand a year before I was out there and although she now realised who she was looking at, again there was absolutely no doubt in Michaela's mind that she was looking at a picture that could very well be me as I would look in later years. So what now? So many strides forward and yet so many leaps back as well. On paper it claims Ray as being my birth father but I now suspect that was purely incidental.

I further suspect that the reason Ray was named as my father on paper was to keep the rest of the alleged scandal hushed up. The indignity, which although these days is almost insignificant in its worth, being that my mother had an affair and that without doubt my brother and I were the result of that affair. In order to maintain dignity and avoid any humiliation it was decided that Ray would be named as the father in all documentation pertaining to the giving up for adoption and subsequent adoption process. Under the circumstances and taking into consideration that at the time of my birth, society took a very dim view of extra marital affairs and indeed as in my case an even dimmer view of childbirth outside wedlock, my 'family' did the only thing they could at the time to maintain family respectability. So as it stands at the moment I am still none the wiser as to my true parentage but I know I am contented, albeit somewhat confused still, only time will tell whether or not the final truth will out.

However despite the confusion and somewhat uncertainty of all the above information, out of all of that has come to pass I have gained two wonderful sisters who I love more than I could possibly put down on paper. I have a brother who at this juncture I have yet to meet but who is fully aware of my existence and as keen as I am to in due course meet up when time and distance allow, there is a step brother James and his wife Emma both of whom I have met and his sister Louisa who lives in the United Kingdom with their mother Carole. To date I have not met her nor her mother, Clare, Jill and Stephens step mother. As it stands I am not sure what they know of me if anything or indeed whether or not they would want too pursue any form of contact. I would respect that decision wholeheartedly; after all, they have their memories of Ray without me being a part of that. Should they wish that to change then I will always be here. I will be guided by my sisters on that and am happy to

be after all they are my big sisters and I am their little brother, something I absolutely and without reservation take great delight in. I also have nieces and nephews some I have met - Ally and her soon to be husband Travis - and some I haven't, but what I do know is that I am now part of a family who live on the other side of the world and it is the best feeling and without doubt the best experience of my life ever.

Eleven

A Rock and a Hard Place

SO WHERE AM I NOW? Well between a rock and hard place best describes where I am. I have experienced highs and lows of an event that only a few can even imagine. Someone I was talking to just the other day said it must be an incredible experience and you know overall it was just that.

To a certain extent I underwent a transformation from having a family that I grew up with to having an extended family I want to grow old with. I miss my family in Australia every day and I can honestly say that there isn't a day that goes past when I don't wonder what they are doing or where they are. Made easier in some respects, because I have lived in their houses, walked in their shadows and breathed the same air as them but by the same token harder because of it, they are my flesh and blood, from the same gene pool and because of that I have the most incredible feeling of finally belonging. I finally realised that for most of my life there was something missing and that I didn't quite fit in, why I felt more comfortable with my friends from, for want of a better phrase, a working class background rather than the background I had been brought up in. Don't get me wrong, I can adapt as the need arises and can hold my own as the situation dictates. My dad pointed out to me not so long ago that we develop our social standing as result of our genes not by how we are brought up, a definite case of "you can take the boy out of his working class background but you can't take the working class background out of the boy".

I always have and always will fully appreciate my upbringing and am forever grateful to my mum and dad for the unconditional love they gave me as a child. But it is only now that I understand why I was confused and at times frustrated with both myself and my failings in life. I could never understand why my elder sister and younger brother who were both mum and dads natural children would excel whilst I just couldn't aspire to mum and dad's expectations. I used to feel I had failed them. I have a brother and sister who have achieved so much in life and who are both high achievers at director level, with large houses with swimming pools. However, now it is all so very logical and as a result I am so much more comfortable with who I am and what I have achieved in my own life. I was never destined to be a high achiever but I like to think I have excelled in my own field and I am happy with that. I have two fantastic children, a comfortable home and a comfortable lifestyle. For the first time in many years I am contented.

I finally completed and I coin a phrase here from the Disney movie the Lion King, 'the circle of life' I set out all those years ago to find the woman who gave me life and allowed me the opportunity to be who I am today. I achieved that one day in New Zealand in April 2004, I never wanted to replace the family I grew up with or to supplant the people I am proud to call my brothers and sisters. My dad was and always will be just that, my dad, and my very best friend. I owe him and my mum a debt of gratitude. There have been trials and tribulations along the way but isn't there in every family? I am fiercely proud of my family and I am extremely fortunate that I now also have a family in Australia who I am equally proud of. Throughout my life I have been influenced by many people and situations, mainly since I flew the nest and found my own way in the world though. I have experienced the loss of loved ones and those close to me in both tragic circumstances and natural, all of which over time has made my resolve that much stronger and made me appreciate what I now have all the more. There are still many unanswered questions and they are questions that are likely to remain that way as I no longer feel the need to continue to search. I am finally content with my life and where I came from and where I am now heading. Most stories finish with the phrase 'The End' but not this time, for me and my family both old and new this is just 'The Beginning'

Or so I thought, without any preconception of how my life was about to turn out, with a brutal wrench, my wife decided to up and leave me and the children to live with someone else. My fairytale story had just turned into a nightmare and all the new beginnings and future of new found happiness and contentment were blown completely out of the water. The children and I had to cope without a mother and wife. By an extraordinary twist of fate, I was now experiencing the feelings and agonies that my Ray must have experienced all those years ago when Sally told him she was leaving home for someone else and leaving him with the children. My former wife had been my rock, my complete and utter support and I had thought the love of my life. Like many other couples before and since, we had, over the last twenty one years since we first met, had our rocky patches and I fully admitted to mistakes on my behalf which were completely unjustified and totally and completely wrong. I had pushed my luck way too far and across boundaries that should probably never have been crossed. It would have been easy to make excuses for it all and proportion the blame elsewhere. It would have been too easy to blame my childhood and my discovery of my adoption for turning me into the kind of person I became although I strongly believe that as a result of what I discovered all those years ago when I was thirteen made me want more than I could ever have and I spent a long time looking for something that I thought was never there, a place of perfection where I could do no wrong and everybody loved me, a place to belong. That place had always been there in front of me I was just never able to appreciate it and as a result I ended up losing everything that was precious to me at the time. I obviously retained the complete love and support of my children and to them I will be forever grateful for what they gave me especially in the first few weeks of separation because to be completely honest if I may, without them I would probably have been in a place far removed from here desperate and alone and possibly somewhere less corporeal than where I am now.

As for my married life, I thought we had worked through the issues in our marriage completely and in the last two years had made in roads to a better life together and like a lot of couples, I had always had visions of us being together until the day we died, watching our children grow and mature and spreading their wings. This it seems was not the case and in my former wife's own words she had just been going through the motions. She also believed that my journey of discovery and finding of my family had an impact on our marriage as well; she alleged that it had taken over my life and was my sole focus.

At the time of the break up I was left completely broken and shattered; the pain I felt was like nothing I had ever felt in my life. I thought I had felt anguish when those I loved have died in the past. But nothing prepared me for what I felt then, my heart, my head and my whole body ached for the woman I had once been proud to call my wife and the mother of my children. I now faced a life without her, alone and desolate and at the time of writing this I had no idea where my future was headed other than with my children beside me and the long drawn out process and agony of separation and divorce. When I set out on this journey I never imagined that my life would turn out as it now had. Some may want to ask 'was it worth it?' Until that day, yes it had been, every damn minute of it but now? Well that's a different story to be completely honest; I had started to wish I had never laid eyes on that damned adoption certificate thirty years ago knowing what I know now. That said I thought I had loved my former wife completely and utterly, there is no denying that she had been my life and my stability and got me to where I was and for that I perhaps should be forever grateful to her. However she felt I was never completely there for her as I should have been both as a husband and as a father to our children; For that I paid the ultimate price and at the time it was a very heavy burden to bear. But bear it I did, and if I had never loved anyone again then I would have been eternally grateful for having been given the opportunity to know someone such as her.

But, as with most people faced with astonishing situations life moves on and time is a great healer. I have been fortunate to the extreme that I have met my soul mate and have found love again, stronger than before and more complete than before. We met in W.H. Smith in Canterbury, Kent in the Christmas of 2005, we got talking about a book that both of us just happened to be looking at and I suggested we continue our conversation over coffee and the rest as they say is history. My happiness is complete and without reservation, I love her wholly and completely like no-one ever before and have no doubt that we are destined to spend the rest of our lives together, wherever that may be.

The absolute love of my life is Michaela, she knows how I feel about her, I know how she feels about me and for once my life is complete. We have our children and our families and their unconditional love and, of course, each other. We were married on February 18th 2007 in St Lucia, it was an idyllic setting and the most perfect day for us both. It was our day and one we will never forget, just us, on a beach, on Pigeon Island with two witnesses and the Minister directing the marriage. That day and the evening after when we had the best table in the house at a restaurant overlooking the marina will stay in my memories forever. I now have an even further expanded family with the addition of Michaela's children Lee, Lauren and Drew who I care about as much as Damian and Tamara and I have become a proud Granddad too with the arrival of Georgia and Harry who are Laurens children. It has been an extraordinary journey from beginning to end with some unexpected twists but if the truth be known, I wouldn't have missed it for the world.

Twelve

In Retrospect

ON OCCASION I WILL sit down and review everything that occurred with regard to my epic journey to the other side of the world and will question what I did and more importantly, how I did what I did. There will always be the burning questions in the back of my mind, in particular 'what if?' I would be lying to myself if I didn't admit to feelings of frustration; despair and anger - no doubt all part of the process - and a feeling of a need and want to turn the clock back to those last few moments when I met mum and dad for the first time. I would be the first to admit that I was advised on more than one occasion that the initial meeting with them should be on my own, on neutral territory and without the rest of the family I now feel that the all the feelings and emotions that should have been apparent at the first meeting were very possibly muted and withheld as a result of the fact that I failed to heed the warnings and concerns of those I spoke to up until that point. However, it was a decision that I, and I alone, made and no matter what happens now I can never change that moment. There is every chance that things would have turned out completely different to the way they did. We would have had the opportunity to explore our feelings and emotions without the added distractions of me having to ensure my family were happy, settled and comfortable in a strange environment. That is not a criticism of my family in any way, shape or form but I perhaps should have been more assertive in my convictions and insisted way back, when mum and I had spoken initially of our plans, that we stay in a hotel and I had arranged to meet them elsewhere.

So what do I do now? How could I justify going back again and relive everything again? Could I go back again? On the one hand yes I could, damn right I could, Sally is my mother, my flesh and blood, as it would seem now is Ted. Both gave me life and I am a part of them as much as they are a part of me. But how could I go back again? After all the comments from both myself and them in the time after we got home could I justify the expense, the risk of going through more agony and mental torment? They are a twenty-four hour flight away on the other side of the world;

it's not a case of jumping into the car and heading off down the motorway and knocking on the front door. However, there are occasions when I will sit and look at photographs of the house and the land where they live and still are as far as I am aware and wonder what if? But on the other hand I would have to say no - but perhaps that is just the coward in me coming out after all like any human being, I have a fear of rejection and having experienced it once how could I go through that again and be comfortable in myself with it? I have anger and in order to proportion blame I place it wholly on their shoulders which is possibly the most selfish thing I could do when it was a totally unique, highly charged emotional situation that we were all involved in and all responsible for how it turned out.

I am the most fortunate man in the world in that I have the complete and utter love and support of Michaela, who has a completely different perspective on everything that took place all those months ago. She is very perceptive and recognises that there is an awful lot left undone in New Zealand and a degree of pent up anger on my behalf with how things have been left. In her own words, she points out that perhaps we all lost sight of the importance of that first meeting and our own needs to be alone for the first few hours or even days and as a result we caused irreparable damage to a highly emotional and evocative meeting that would have brought massive feelings to a head after so many years. There would have been hidden feelings and thoughts on both sides that were repressed as a result of how we allowed that first meeting to develop.

Who knows, perhaps it is not too late to repair broken hearts and feelings? I am overwhelmed by the complete willingness of Michaela to help and support me through all that has happened and all that is yet to come. She is prepared to sacrifice so much for me to put my mind at rest once and for all. Even to the extent of suggesting that we do fly to the other side of the world, even if it is just for a few days, at the expense on missing out on few years foreign holidays if that's what it takes. She also reminded me of the importance of counselling, something I had never taken into consideration since returning to the UK. After all, I had the full support of Social Services prior to leaving the UK the first time round and have maintained a link with Jane. I should take advantage of the services they provide and will, without question take benefit from those services again, particularly should Michaela and I decide to follow our hearts and decide to travel to the other side of the world to finally get the final chapter some closure.

Part Two - 2009

Thirteen

It's Too Late

I NEVER IMAGINED I WOULD have to write a second edition of my book however so much has happened since the inception of edition one that I feel I have to share it with you. As the saying goes, 'the best laid schemes of mice and men'. From Robert Burns' poem *To a Mouse*, 1786, things were not about to go my way. I deliberated and anguished for far too long. I was at home on my own one September evening in 2008 when there was a knock at the front door, upon opening I was surprised to see my Sergeant on the doorstep asking to come in – he was in uniform so a sense of foreboding came upon me – I led him into the lounge and there was the usual small talk about work and then he came to the point as to why he had descended upon me at home. He asked me if I knew someone called Don Crosby who was an old shipmate of my fathers on HMS Arethusa. I confirmed I had met him just prior to visiting New Zealand when we had spoken about my father and the pending visit to meet my parents for the first time. My sergeant stated in that case he had some bad news, apparently my mother had passed away after a short illness in a hospital in Rotorua , but to add to the tragedy my father who was absolutely devoted to her had decided to take his own life to be with her. I had to come to terms with the death of my mother, which despite everything that had passed, I found difficult to come to terms with. I am not ashamed to admit that on hearing the news I was devastated and when Michaela arrived home after the news had been broken to me she found me in floods of tears, all I could say to her was 'my mum's dead' she was a tower of strength and consoled me with love and understanding until I was able to tell her what had happened. She was as devastated as I was and the obvious question came up with regard to would we be going to New Zealand for the funeral and to be there for my father.

At the time of my mothers death he had sent two emails one of which was to an old friend of his in Spain the gist of which stated that 'the light in his life had gone out'.

He had sent them without taking into account the time difference in Spain and fortunately the recipient in Spain had decided that evening to check his emails prior to retiring for the night. What follows is a transcript of what happened taken from an email between Paul (Spain), Brian (Auckland) and Don (UK):

Where do I start.............this morning I decided to go in late to work and check my e-mail before leaving home. Thank God I did....................As I was on line an e-mail from Paul in Spain arrived...........................Paul had JUST got an e-mail from Ted Harman saying his wife Sally had just died and he was going to join her !!!!!!!!!!!!!! Paul did not know what to do..........Ted and Sally lived on their own out in the ' wop-wops' outside of Rotorua, I think you may have visited them when in NZ...............They live about 5 hours way from me....................Anyway, I found Ted's phone number and I had asked him for his address a while ago......I thought I would see if he would answer the phone and he did !..........he was very calm and stated he was about to e-mail me with his last request !!!.........I cannot remember all that was said after that , other than he said he had all the pills lined up ready to take and then join Sally..................I asked him to delay for another hour and think more etc, etc, etc, and I would phone back.......shit, I thought, what the bloody hell do I do?..............I hung up and dialled 111 and got the cops to him in time to get him to hospital and pump him dry...................I spoke to the hospital a couple of hours ago and his nurse told me he is settled at the moment and under "watch", they will have the ward social worker talk with him tomorrow. He is 77years old I think.

So, Ted is in the best place for the time being. .... Now Don, the main reason for this e-mail........................... They do not seem to be able to trace any family or friends, seems they kept themselves to themselves and are concerned for him about this........................ Paul in Spain seems to think they might have twins that were adopted out and met up with again a few years ago and fell out with again and maybe another son some where in the UK (however he's not sure about any of this). Is there any way you could quietly find out any more about Ted's/Sally's family through the Arethusa Old Boys Association?

Sorry to place extra work on you Don, but if you can help, it might get a result.

I think at the moment Ted will not thank me for stopping him doing what he wanted to do this morning, but hopefully he will come right and enjoy the rest of his days .I will contact the hospital down there again to check on progress tomorrow.

Don, the above is for your eyes and info only, I am concerned we do not spread Ted's problems more than need be without his permission, I am sure you will understand this. He of course does not know I have contacted you, but I think he will need support from anywhere in the coming times.

I have never met Ted or Sally, though I have spoken once last year on the phone with them and of course e-mails back and forth. The bond is as always the Arethusa.................

Having been rushed into hospital and purely by luck, because of time differences and the gut instinct of old shipmates, Rotorua Police and the hospital staff he survived the ordeal. Mentally and physically he was understandably in a very feeble condition, but with more than adequate care from the nursing staff and visits from the Brian his old shipmate from Auckland he slowly reached a degree of normality in his life again. Brian was a lifeline and my only contact in New Zealand and I am indebted to him for what he did both at the time of the tragedy and subsequently. He travelled down to Rotorua to see my father and emailed me afterwards to keep me up to date with his condition, you may remember that when I left New Zealand back in 2004 our parting had not been on good terms, so I was in turmoil with regard to how to make contact – I did however ring the hospital, spoke to his nurse and left a message for him so he was aware I had been in touch. Below is the email from Brian after he had visited my father:

Got down to Rotorua yesterday afternoon and was able to provide the hospital with a few more details which they were pleased to get.... After a chat with his nurse in mental-health, I was shown into Ted's room and was very pleased to find him, stable, with it and appearing to have all his marbles

We had a long talk and he has come to grips now with Sally passing away and now cannot wait to get home and start "clearing up and getting on with job's at home ". This of course is great positive news I think..............he did say if he could of got hold of me Tuesday/Wednesday he might have killed me though !!!

But he now thanks everyone who had a hand in stopping him doing the deed...............Seems when the cop's got there (he said very, very quickly after my call), he was on the last bottle of pills ,while they had him shot off to hospital to get pumped out, the cop's took all his gun's away with them.

Ted hopes to be sent home tomorrow, but talking to his nurse, he is still under 24/7 watch and he will be spoken to by the powers that be again tomorrow (Monday) and they will decide........he may be sent home "on leave", but in any event, she said he will go no where until "support "has been put in place for him..

Arrangements have now been made for Sally's funeral, but not a date. I am sorry to say, I will not be able to return south for this, Ted knows this and understands why as I have explained things to him

As I say, I was with him yesterday and shot out and got him newspaper and smokes etc, which cheered him up even more and I decided to stay over night in Rotorua at a motel, so I could see him this morning (Sunday) before driving home. This morning I took him in the Sunday papers, he was bright as a button, and so in the end, I left him in the care of the lovely staff at mental-health. A great result at the end of a hectic week

He has no one local to visit him, but the lady who lives near by is keeping in touch with him in hospital.

On Friday ,as he was so concerned about things at home and with no one being there, they took him home for a while (under watch),and then brought him back ...I thought that was really good of them to do that. (Ted tells me, while at home he managed to sneak a couple of tots down, while his minder looked the other way. He was able to send some e-mails too.)I gave Ted a copy of your last e-mail to me. I know from the way he acted that he very much appreciated your concern and thoughts and he spoke fondly of you to me. Can't think of anything else to pass on at present, please contact me at any time if I can help in any way.

It would appear from the above email that there was every chance that bridges once thought to have long been burnt could be rebuilt – so I duly emailed my father. I had been informed was now back at home having been given the all clear and was starting to rebuild his life without Sally and I as the dutiful son was back in his life concerned as any son would be about his welfare and wellbeing. However I never received a reply and was now left with the anguish of deciding whether or not I was going to be able to attend my mother's funeral? Michaela was fully supportive about everything including the possibility of a trip to the other side of the world. It was not to be however, my father in his wisdom had decided that he didn't want anyone to attend the funeral – despite the wishes of various siblings including Jill, Stephen and myself who had expressed our wishes to attend. I had to ring Jill to inform her that our mother had passed away as neither Jill nor Clare nor Stephen had been informed of Sally's passing and it was then I realised that there were still issues that were far from resolved in terms of how my father felt about what had occurred four years previously.

Fourteen

The Surprises Keep Coming

WHILST STILL COMING TO terms with what had happened and whether or not, despite everything, I should go to New Zealand to pay my last respects to my mother another revelation unfolded before me in the form of an email on once again Friends Reunited, The sender was Arthur Harman and was as follows:

Hi Andy, I hope you will forgive the unorthodox approach but I don't have an up to date email address for you. I gather you have heard the news from NZ and you have my condolences. Perhaps you could call me and we can share what information we have? Regards Arthur Harman

Ted's son from his first marriage, I had known that he had three children before me but he had never talked about them and never wanted too either which out of respect I did not pursue. But now I had been presented an opportunity to meet more siblings from the 'other side of the family'. We of course had a lot to talk about but we had to put that to one side for the time being as we had to deal with events that had been unfolding in New Zealand.

Arthur understandably was not planning on going to New Zealand but he was however in contact with our father both by phone, a feat in itself as he is deaf, he had forwarded my email address to our father, but still he didn't acknowledge the emails I sent him enquiring after his welfare and health. In the end I had to rely on Arthur for updates which were incredibly frustrating from my perspective as I was desperate for contact and genuinely hurt that he had not contacted me. Arthur and I spoke at some length in between updates from New Zealand and I was once again enthralled by information that was relating to my previous life. I learned that I had two sisters, one who lives a mere 35 miles from me and another who lived in Sussex not far from Arthur. They were both aware of my existence and that Arthur had contacted me but had expressed no wish to make contact, as is only right and proper in these cases I respected their views and left it at that, but who knows in the fullness of time things may change and I can finally meet the rest of the family. It transpired that Arthur's mother had never married again after being divorced by Ted and so like my own parents had no more children since we were born. Arthur also informed me that at the time his mother would have quite happily taken us on and brought us up with the rest of the family – that was how much she was devoted to Ted. However, as was the case with Ray (Sally's ex-husband) who had offered the same it was not to be and the die was cast. Arthur also informed me that Alistair and I had been separated at some point and one of us, although it is unknown which of us, was looked after by persons unknown just up the road from where Arthur grew up. It must have only been for a brief while though as there is no record of it in any of the documents I have seen to date. So close to my family and yet so far and it was to be 45 years before I was to meet them face to face for the first time.

As you would expect a meeting had to be arranged and so one Sunday in October accompanied with torrential rain Michaela, Drew and I headed down to Sussex. We duly arrived at Arthur's house and another surreal meeting evolved. We met Arthur and his wife Amanda and young son, Drew and his son hit it off almost immediately, I suspect the Play Station 3 helped cement the friendship and so the adults were left to peruse photographs and documents at our leisure. I was astounded at what I saw, it was unequivocal as to who my father was. I saw photographs that at times had me believe I was looking in a mirror – photographs of my father in the Royal Navy at the age of 16 which other than the date of the uniform could have been me in uniform when I joined the Royal Navy decades later. I have a copy of that photograph and no matter who I show it too and ask who they think it is, the answer is always the same – 'why it's you of course'.

We had a great afternoon, sharing our views about my mother and our father, unsurprisingly Arthur and his wife Amanda had experienced a similar experience to mine when they visited them in New Zealand and we both more or less came to the same conclusion that there was a degree of selfishness on their part. However I had slowly mellowed over the years and had perhaps made excuses for their shortcomings whereas Arthur had been in regular contact with our father up until my mothers death and since and was still of the opinion that they deserved what they got to a degree. In retrospect I guess he was right, they had chosen their path in life and in doing so they had both abandoned children from previous marriages and their own children from their affair to boot, not only that having abandoned me and Alistair they then disappeared to the other side of the world and got married and lived out their existence blissfully unaware of the carnage they had left behind. Although I still find it hard to believe that they could have forgotten about us all – but as for guilt? I sincerely doubt it ever came into the equation, or did it? There was only one person who could answer that but I doubted more and more that I was ever likely to find out in the not to distant future.

I noted an element of resentment with Arthur about our father, but it was in my opinion completely justified and overwhelmingly understandable. As a result of my mother and our father's actions, he had lost a father at a very young age and it had been my mother that took his father away from the family home. Any child would be bitter, hurt, angry and confused no matter what age they were and those feelings run deep and will do for the rest of their life. Much in the same way Clare, Jill and Stephen had felt but from the other side of the equation. A lighter note of the afternoon having had lunch was whilst looking at some family photographs on the kitchen wall; I noticed a face amongst the family that looked familiar but that I couldn't initially place and then it came to me. I was looking at Kate Winslet star of Titanic, The Reader, Sense and Sensibility, Little Children and Iris to name a few of her achievements. To cut a long story short as it's not mine to tell, Amanda was related to Kate Winslet through her side of the family. It is always pleasant to hear someone else's story of finding family and subsequent connections and a timely reminder that I am not alone in my quest for information about family roots and relatives hitherto unidentified.

And so after an afternoon of untold revelations Arthur took me on a drive around his and in a roundabout way my home town. He drove me to a street not far from where he now lives and showed me the flat that my mother and our father had rented for a while when they first embarked upon their relationship forty five years previously. It was a strange experience seeing it in a way; after all it was where both my parents had spent time together before embarking upon their life together without me. We talked further about Sally and Susan and about how their lives had turned out since that fateful day and of course Arthur's mother. She had known I was coming down to see Arthur but had no desire to meet me something I could fully understand after all I was the result of an affair that her husband had which left her on her own with three children to bring up. From a personal point of view I would love to meet her one day but only on her terms and I would certainly not begrudge one iota if she chooses not to, but as time goes by one never knows. I was left though with an overwhelming feeling of sadness when I realised that no matter what had happened all those years ago, she obviously had feelings for Ted that ran very deep and had always remained so and to that end had chosen not to get married again unlike Ray who had.

So we left Sussex still in torrential rain and headed home, my mind buzzing with all the new found information, with promises made to get together again soon with Arthur and his family and get copies of all photographs and documents that we had seen that day.

Fifteen

The Unbelievable Happens

TIME MARCHES ON AND waits for no man and before we know it Christmas had been and gone, despite phone calls and emails Arthur and I had not got together again despite a number of attempts to do so. In March I received the following email from Brian in Auckland as he had been down to visit my father;

Well for this first time, I travelled south to visit (and check on) Ted, not in hospital (as the last two trips), BUT............... at his home out in the wop-wops.

It was great to see him at his home and in much better shape than before. With the aid of Google and their trip-map, I located his place with out any problems other than the country road upgrades which slowed me down some what. Yesterday was not too hot weather wise, so that made the four hour trip down quite easy.

Ted, for his age (I think 78 now) is of course living on his own after Sally passing away last year. He is doing very well and gets visits from his nurse still and now others not too far away are keeping an eye on him from time to time as well, he tells me............................... He was bright and in good cheer, enjoying a couple of red wines at mid-day :-) He is looking forward to getting new hearing aids on Monday for which he will have to go into Rotorua.

I remembered to take down my old Arethusa photos and leaving certificate and he enjoyed looking through them with me, even though he was on board long before me. I had loaned him my copy of "Painting the Last Post" (written about life on the Arethusa by another old boy), when he was in hospital and he said he did enjoy that too.

Well, that's the latest on Ted.....all good..........................me, I am going to crash with a couple of cold ones now after the drive home this afternoon.

Enjoy what's left of your weekend

I was still getting no response to my emails and phoning was now out of the question due to his hearing. However Arthur was keeping me up to speed with his general health as was Brian so I wasn't quite out of the loop yet. However the next email from Brian was to floor me completely. Michaela and I had been away for the weekend at the birth of our latest grandchild so when we got home I thought I had better check our emails before retiring for the night and this is what I found from Brian dated 16th May 2009;

Last night I was woken by a phone call from the Rotorua Police, with the very sad news that Ted had passed away in while in hospital. The police wanted any info I had on Ted's family so they could contact them.......I gave them your e-mail addresses. They requested I did not contact you for a few hours to give them a chance to make contact first. I did not have your phone numbers. Hopefully they have got through to you now. Otherwise, I am sorry to be the bearer of such sad news.

I will contact the hospital and Ted's nurse tomorrow (Monday) to find out what arrangements have or will be made. As you know, since Sally passed away, I have travelled down to see him several times and was pleased to see him improve with every trip. I would like to travel down one last time, to say farewell, so should you learn when his funeral will be before me, please let me know. I live four hours away, so cannot help with Ted's local affairs, but please contact me if you think I can help in any way at all.

Suffice to say I hadn't heard from anyone let alone the New Zealand Police or the Rotorua Hospital. I obviously heard from Arthur the following morning who confirmed the news. We both agreed that it was inevitable as once my mother had passed away it was only a matter of time before our father would follow – they were devoted to each other after all. Thankfully there was no repetition of an attempt to take his own life, his general health just deteriorated over the preceding seven months since my mother died. He felt he had nothing to live for without her so for him it was a kind of blessing in disguise and he was now where he wanted to be all those months ago with 'the light of his life'.

I was at a loss with regard to what to do, again I found myself anguishing about flying out to New Zealand.

Michaela was adamant that we should go and I started to make plans despite the fact he had not been in contact since the death of my mother. Here was an opportunity to pay my respects to both my parents, it was about then that the reality started to kick in. My birth parents had now passed away, I had lost every chance of putting right what went wrong all those years ago the frustration and anguish I started to experience was something I had never expected and never considered from the outset of my journey, yes there had been every chance that they had passed away before I found them, but they hadn't. Add to the fact that not only had I found my birth mother alive and well but also my birth father who was married to my mother – I had been fortunate to experience the euphoria of the initial search and discovery that some adopted people never have, what happened in New Zealand on meeting them had faded and I had started to come to terms with what happened even to the point of re-visiting them to start over again. That now could never happen and the realisation was only just starting to dawn on me.

Sixteen

The Pain and the Agony

HAVING BEEN THROUGH THE process of discovery and meeting family members previously unknown and the exhilaration of all that had happened, it was probably inevitable that I was going to come back down to earth with a bump. However I never expected it to be so colossal. As you will have read my life from then on experienced massive highs and incredible lows and amazing discoveries along the way, all of which I will be forever grateful for as it gave me an identity something I never felt I had ever had. However I was not prepared for how it was going to leave me mentally

The realisation of what had occurred since my initial discovery was beginning to have a profound affect on my personal life. As previously mentioned my first marriage had broken up, although in all respects that was a blessing in disguise as I would never have met Michaela and for that I will be eternally grateful. I had been made redundant at work from my role of Operational Supervisor at the same time a role I had been happy in and one that fulfilled my aspirations with Thames Valley Police, not a major issue but relevant. I was on anti-depressants and had started to drink more than I used to – even to the point of hiding bottles of wine from Michaela – I was on a slippery slope to self destruction and hadn't even realised it. At the time I wasn't even aware what the cause was. I was starting to lash out verbally at the people I most cared about albeit not everyday, but I was turning from a placid, caring husband, dad and step-dad into quite frankly someone no-one wanted to be around.

I became increasingly angry about my childhood and found myself constantly thinking about how and why I had so many regrets about events in my life, already catalogued in the earlier chapters in this book. I had begun to question everything about my existence, my relationship with my adopted family which by now was at an all time low. I had begun to cut myself off completely from them including my dad. I had made my mind up that I didn't want to have anything to do with any of them ever again. Every time I had spoken to them or met up with them I argued with them accusing them of how much I felt let down by them, how they refused to acknowledge that Michaela was my wife and my whole life, yet still they continued to treat my ex-wife as part of the family, more so than Michaela which infuriated me then as much as it does now. I knew my relationship with them would never be the same again or as it used to be and I didn't care – I was now in self destruct mode after all.

A notable low point was at my brother Duncan's house where we had been invited for New Year – I had managed to down at least one bottle of wine and was attempting to have a pleasant and civil conversation with my dad in the presence of my brother, his wife and Michaela. I challenged my dad about his behaviour towards my ex-wife to which he replied in no uncertain terms that I was being preposterous and I should grow up. I just exploded and raged at everyone in the room, Duncan's wife treated me with utter disdain and told me that it was her house and that I should calm down, which of course just made matters worse, in my opinion I was still being treated as I had been when I was a child. In the end I broke down and left the room, Michaela hot on my heels, as ever my only true support, full of care love and understanding. I just wanted to get out of the house and head for home, not a wise move considering I intended to drive and one I quickly realised was not one of my better decisions. Suffice to say we left the next day as soon as we could and have not been back since and there are no plans to do so.

I started to question everything I had ever done in my life since the time I had made my discovery. Analysing certain events and realising how possibly my life could have been different had I not made my discovery. Had I been treated so differently from the rest of my siblings because of what I had done? To me the answer was glaringly obvious; yes I had and still continued to be to this day. So many missed opportunities that had been denied to me by my parents in particular my mum, everybody in my family bar me was allowed to do whatever they wanted with their lives anything I had suggested was always met with a negative response. I have come to the conclusion that because I had dared to find out that I had been adopted and worse still questioned my parents about the circumstances and to that end had forced their hand into admitting everything, despite my dad's protests that they had never kept it a secret. I had opened a Pandora's Box that was to change my life from thereon in. Whether it was consciously or subconsciously I now felt that my mum in particular felt some kind of rejection and to that end treated me differently and in turn, again subconsciously, rejected me.

I rightly or wrongly didn't leave it there and continued my quest for more information and as a result probably made the gulf between us wider. In my naivety I saw nothing wrong in what I was doing and I thought supporting my mum whilst my dad was away working, in essence being the man of the house that I was being appreciated. The rest of my siblings were off doing what they wanted to do whether it be out with friends or off to university whilst I stayed at home with mum helping around the house decorating or gardening or just being company of an evening whilst she marked books or exam papers. I epitomized the archetypal mummy's boy, in retrospect I was a fool, but hindsight is a wonderful thing is it not? Had I known then what I know now would I have pursued the course I did? It was only when my career choices were denied me, as detailed in chapter one, that the cracks started to show and I started to kick out culminating in my career choice of the Royal Navy in order to escape the oppression I felt I was being subjected to at home.

Life never really got any better, I walked into a marriage which again was a means of escape and was something my mum and dad totally disagreed with so again of course I followed it through as a way of getting back at them. So young and so naïve yet blind to what I was doing to myself I continued to blunder through life, bored with my marriage and my life having now left the navy and being deceived into having one child and coerced into having another, although it goes without saying I will never, ever regret having them and will love them unconditionally forever no matter what. They helped keep me grounded in so many ways and in particular my daughter. However I sought solace elsewhere and it's only now that I realise I was looking for someone who actually cared about me for who I was and who would love me back. I wanted someone to understand me and listen to me. I failed in everything I set out to do with regard to a career never achieving anything of any note. I had no skills, no qualifications and no self esteem as such. Thames Valley Police restored my self esteem but I was still adamant that I was going to discover my roots and continued to push and press for information until I finally achieved my goal in 2003.

I thought after all those years life could and would only get better and for a while it seemed to do just that – despite what happened in New Zealand. But after all the initial euphoria and exhilaration it nosedived dramatically.

I became angry with life and turned on the people I most cared about including Michaela. At times all I wanted to do was get away and be on my own to wallow in my own self pity and would start arguments over the most trivial of things just so I had the excuse to leave. Invariably I would find myself sat in a hotel room with a bottle of whisky and being thoroughly miserable, wondering why I was there and wrestling with my conscience. When the only place I desperately wanted to be was at home with Michaela the only person who truly understood me, cared about me and loved me passionately. Yet she was the one who was bearing the brunt of my bitterness and anger. Was it any wonder she was beginning to question where our relationship was headed?

For the sake of my wife and for my own sanity I made the decision to finally do something about it. I decided to cut out everything that had been the root cause of how I now felt and made the momentous decision to cut my siblings out of my life for good, some of them had their reasons for doing the same to me, in particular my twin brother but from my perspective it suited me absolutely fine.

It is nearly two years now since I spoke to any of them or had anything to do with them. For a long time my relationship with my dad was frosty and non-committal. He had now moved to the South Coast nearer my younger brother so any responsibility I once had was now well and truly over. We still spoke over the phone occasionally but I was very much on my guard and never discussed my family in detail or what plans we had. I have become an extremely closed person. I trust no-one in my adopted family and very, very few people outside it. He finally realised that I had no interest in what my siblings were doing and no longer discussed them or tried to tell me what they were all up to. Although being in his eighties he did sometimes forget and mentioned them in passing. I on the other hand never asked him about them. I can't remember when I last spoke to Clare or Jill, although we do still exchange Christmas cards. I have lost touch with Arthur ever since the death of our father. But suffering rejection is nothing new to me now. Neither of his sisters expressed a wish to have contact with me which is absolutely their choice and I fully respect their wishes.

I had been rejected by my mother and father at birth and now again at their death. I believe now that throughout Ted's life he had harboured some incredible guilt about Arthur and his sisters and their mother and on the death of my mother he was able to try and find some resolution with Arthur and his other children. I was not to be included in that and that hurt more than I can even start to explain. Having spent so many years, time and effort to trace them it would seem no it was to no avail. I have been to hell and back as a result of what I did and lost so much on the way.

Don't get me wrong I enjoyed the discoveries and the experiences, I just never realised how much damage I had caused to myself personally. For me life began again

Christmas 2006 when I met Michaela, I realise now that was a significant turning point in my life, despite the agonies I still had to endure with my own demons, I only came through them because of Michaela's strength and enduring love and faith in me. My only family now are Michaela and our kids and that is the way it will remain. I spent my whole life trying to be someone I could never be and to impress people who could never be impressed. I trusted them and believed in them and because of them my faith in humanity has been severely tested. Now that may seem to some as extremely harsh but it is my decision and one that has relieved me of an incredible amount of pain and anguish. I can without hesitation say that the first forty three years of my life have transpired to be more troubled than I had realised and it would seem most of it was caused by my own actions. But also by the actions and attitude of others, I am sure that there are those that would argue otherwise but on reflection I am not so sure.

Chapter 17

This Has to Be How It Ends.

2019: I HAVE TO END THIS but before I do, this is where my story has got too. For those who have stuck with me so far I thank you, I did say right at the beginning it was going to be a roller coaster of a ride. I hope I haven't disappointed the thrill seeker in you thus far.

So, to date, I have found and met two sisters in Australia, my parents in New Zealand, my half-brother and his family in Sussex, upset and subsequently been ostracised by my adopted family in Buckinghamshire. Got divorced from someone I thought I could trust and believe in. Found and married my absolute soulmate and the absolute love of my life. Expanded the boundaries of my family beyond anything I could ever have imagined was possible, found a career I could be proud of and have excelled at. Life couldn't possibly get better than this……. Or could it?

Cast your mind back if you will to Perth 2004, in passing I met James and Emma Lingwood who had just moved out to Australia and were in the process of buying their first house. James is Claire, Jill's and Stephens half-brother, Raymond and Carole's son. Carole being the second wife of Raymond after my mother left him with three children to bring up alone. They also had a daughter, Louisa who still lived in Surrey in the UK.

So what on earth has this all got to do with me and my story you I hear you say? Well read on dear reader and see where we go from here, one last ride, one last revelation and I have no doubt there will be those of us who will want to say 'I knew it' and those of us who will be saying 'No way, really, but how' etc., etc.

Jill and I have seen each other quite a bit of late given that she lives on the other side of the world. She and her new partner Brendan have been to stay in the UK for extended periods over the past couple of years which has given us a lot of time to catch up on past events. Both Clare and David (her husband) are at the end of a phone, text or Skype and of course everybody's favourite Facebook and Messenger keeps us in touch on a more or less weekly basis.

When I met Clare in 2004, unbeknown to me both she and Jill had been speaking over the phone about certain mannerisms that they had both identified separately but which had set their minds racing to certain conclusions. Those being that I was displaying traits of their father, Raymond, which were to their mind confirming what they had always thought and brought into serious doubt my thoughts about my actual parentage.

On my birth certificate it stated that Raymond Lingwood was my father, but Social Services had told me Ted Harmon was indeed my father as told to them by my mother Sally. To that end it was assumed that the only obvious reason that Raymond had been listed as my father was to promote an air of decency surrounding the stigma of what would otherwise be two illegitimate babies. Bearing in mind that even in the early 1960's, there was still a certain shame to be had if you had children out of wedlock and god forbid as the result of an affair.

Then there was something that Michaela had seen or in actual fact not seen that I had been oblivious too at the time, but when looked at retrospectively was glaringly obvious.

Arthur and I bore no resemblance to each other in any way shape or form. Compare photos of me with Clare and Jill and there are facial features that are so obvious in particular the chin and around the eyes. With Arthur there is nothing that obvious. Perhaps he realised as well, which may go some way to explaining his extraordinary behaviour when our father died. Initially we communicated via email and phone about the funeral, even flying out together to New Zealand then nothing. The next thing I know the funeral has been done and dusted and once again I have been rejected and excommunicated. I received a package in the post one day containing a few documents and photos of my mother but nothing of my father. I emailed Arthur a couple of times asking for copies of documents pertaining to our father but never heard anything more then or now.

It slowly dawned on me that something was clearly not as it seemed, but for the life of me I couldn't work out what, despite certain misgivings I was having. Sure I came up with numerous theories but still refused to ignore what was written in black and white:

'Ted Harmon – Father'

After all, my mother wouldn't lie; she had assured me and reassured me that she and my father had often whiled away the best part of forty years of birthdays and Christmases wondering what I had been up to and where I had been all this time, why they had even sent a letter to an adoption agency in the UK asking to be informed if anyone should make enquiries about them. But still there was my birth certificate which stated something completely different to what she and my father were telling me.

In 2016 David, my sister Clare's husband messaged me and in passing mentioned that James, my half-brother, was flying to the UK to take part in the Ride London Cycle Race. On a whim I messaged James and said as he was coming over why we didn't arrange to meet up at some point, although I was conscious he was only over for a matter of days just for the race. A date was agreed but as time was going to be against us due to the race we decided that we would meet up at a local restaurant in Surrey with the added bonus that Louisa, his sister and and her new husband would also be there.

Surrey, the stockbroker belt and the site of Box Hill which was destined to be part of the route James would be cycling and incidentally was also part of the 2012 Summer Olympics cycling road race as well.

I was excited at the prospect of putting faces to names and adding to my ever increasing family, but I couldn't have been more wrong as to how things were destined to pan out.

I of course had spoken with both Jill and Clare about Louisa but had never really given it much thought as she was their half-sister as much as James was their half-brother. James on the other hand had been in my friends list on Facebook for a few years now. After all he lived in the same area of Western Australia as Clare namely Perth and as is usually the way of things it seems only natural that friends of friends and in family lists are added to your list almost as a matter of course these days, well you get the drift.

Lunch progressed after introductions were completed while the conversation turned as it does at first meetings about careers, children and Louisa and her very recent wedding as in just days before the family get together. I would even go as far as to say the first meeting was much the same as my first meetings with Clare and Jill, there was something almost tangible about it all. So much so that we adjourned to Louisa's home to continue what had already begun, there the conversation turned to parents and then the revelation to beat all revelations whilst discussing Raymond.

Both James and Louisa were in no doubt about whom my father was, in fact there had once again been similar conversations as to those had by Clare and Jill in the early days. However the physical evidence was infallible in its self from my wives personal observations and heightened palpability since we had all met over lunch of belonging. Louisa and James both stated that they had no doubt about their belief was that Raymond was my father. If you look at photographs of Louisa, James and I there are undoubtedly physical features that are the same, chins and eyes being the most obvious. This would be an impossibility given the parentage I had been given by Social Services and my mother.

After all consider the facts, if my father was Ted Harman and my mother Sally Harman there is absolutely no possible way I could bear any resemblance to Louisa and James as according to Social Services and my mother James and

Louisa had the same father as Clare, Jill and Stephen but a different mother as Raymond had remarried.

Yet here we were, looking at each other in the flesh so to speak and James and Louisa both saying how much I looked like their father Raymond, bear in mind this was not the first time I had heard this revelation but up until now I had discounted it as out of the question due to the evidence I had been given by to be honest, people and organisations you would think it would be hard to doubt.

Me Louisa and James – 'The penny dropped'

Suddenly it was all making so much sense, cast your mind back to the meeting in New Zealand of my 'parents' and how it all fell apart after the first three days. The day we returned to a silent house and no dinner and the final day when I returned to give them one last chance to no avail and the lone figure of Ted standing on the deck area as I drove away, with no sign of my mother.

Ted and Raymond had worked together and at one point had been friends, which is how he had met my mother whilst still being married to his first wife and mother of Arthur Harman and his two sisters. What Ted had seen on that first day and the whole time I had been there was an image of the man whose wife he had embarked on an affair with. He had been spun a lie from the day Sally fell pregnant with twins, she had still been sleeping and having marital relations with Raymond whilst at the same time sleeping with Ted. Rather than face up to the enormity of what had now occurred she decided to cover it up and made the decision to put us up for adoption.

Raymond knew we were his and had already stated that he would be more than happy to bring us up with Jill, Clare and Stephen but he was denied the opportunity and in doing so I was also denied the opportunity of being brought up with my true siblings.

Ted believed we were his, but as we were the product of an affair and they were now living in a one bedroom flat they were in no position to offer us a happy, comfortable upbringing so 'they' decided the only option was to put us up for adoption.

The reality was Sally knew damn well who the father was but rather than risk losing Ted who she had fallen head over heels in love with and the future she had planned to have with him. She clearly didn't want to risk having to resume a marriage she obviously didn't want with Raymond just because she was now having his twin babies, that was clearly not in her plans whatsoever either.

So the only option was adoption, out of sight and out of mind and no questions asked, bear in mind back in the 1960's there was an air of secrecy around adoptions. There was no question of having to reveal to anyone the circumstances or reasons for the adoption and the mother had the final say. The die was cast and my future decided with no thought of the consequences it would seem.

In the last year I have made a decision now that my story has reached its conclusion, it was always in the back of my mind to make a change but out of respect to my adopted parents I have left it until now to do it.

By deed poll I have changed my name back to my birth name albeit with a subtle difference in that from

Brian Andrew Robert Angus

to

Andrew Simon Raymond Lingwood

My true birth name Simon, my true fathers name Raymond and the name I should have grown up with, Lingwood. It was agreed that I should keep Andrew as that would have been a step too far as everyone knew me as Andrew (Andy) including my family and also out of courtesy to my adopted parents who had called me Andrew anyway. Suffice to say I have told my adopted brothers and sisters of my decision and although my brother Duncan has said 'you will always be my brother no matter what your name is' I have not heard from any of them since.

If I'm honest with myself, it's of no consequence, the chasm has been there all along I have just cut the ropes holding the bridge in place and moved on.

If life had been different and my mother had not acted as selfishly as she had done in order to satisfy her own needs, I would have been brought up with my family, my brothers and sisters and most importantly my father. She denied me that opportunity because it didn't fit her needs. I am glad that I met her, absolutely I am I just won't forgive her for what she did. She went on to have the life she wanted with the man she wanted in a place far away from everyone she had ever come into contact with, her children, her ex-husband and the children she gave up to the authorities which enabled her to live her life by her rules. As a lot of people have judged, she was a mother who clearly had no maternal feelings yet went on to have five children to then just abandon them with no thought or feelings but to satisfy her own needs? We were all fortunate in that three of us were brought up by our father and went on to have a brother and a sister and that two of us were adopted into a family who loved us and nurtured us as their own.

Epilogue

SO THERE YOU HAVE IT; we are now some years down the line from the initial discovery and from the epic journey to the other side of the world. Life can be cruel and as you will have read I went to hell and back for a while as a result of all that happened. I haven't been back to Australia since but that's not because I don't want to, because believe me I do. It's a long way away and that does not make it an inexpensive trip. I want Michaela to meet my sisters because I know they would love her as much as I do and treat her like one of the family unlike my adopted family and more than that I want her to meet them and I know Michaela has a strong desire to go to Australia as she also has family living n Perth, so that's a dividend. Our day will come, that much I do know. It is something we will do whether it is with all our family or just the two of us together. My life has changed dramatically since the inception of my journey of discovery but despite the agonies of late, my life is nothing short of perfect now. I am the happiest at this time than I have ever been and I could ask for no more. I have many people to be grateful too for their support through the good and the bad and for coming into my life. I could list them all here but it would read like a guest list for a wedding. They all know who they are and all I can say is thank you, I will be eternally grateful.

The upside of writing this journal is that other people have benefited from my experiences, one in particular stands out and that is a story told to me by Annie Worrell, a colleague, whose friend as a result of my journey and subsequent book set out on a journey of her own. In Annie's own words;

"I was chatting to you on shift one evening regarding your family history and having been intrigued I subsequently purchased your book. Having read the manuscript of your journey, I felt compelled to discuss this with a good friend of mine who had to give up her first born some years ago. She has never fully recovered from the ordeal and has spent many years trying to trace and locate her natural born son as yet without any margin of success. Your book managed to hit on the many issues that were going through my friends mind at that time and as you had described it so accurately she was emotionally grateful to have been given some possible routes to take that she had not considered before. I truly believe that your book was an inspiration to read and not only highlights the good but also considers the possible heartaches that could be faced. I eagerly await the follow up."

What better reason for writing this book and for me a genuine and gratifying account from someone who benefited from me having written it, if I have achieved a modicum of success and made someone else's journey easier to undertake with an outcome that brings them success and happiness, then my work here is done.

For you who are reading this book and have managed to get this far, I thank you for taking the time to show an interest, I hope you take something away with you as I have from the experiences I have achieved. Live life to the full and remember to live everyday as if it was your last.

Andy Simon Raymond Lingwood

(nee Brian Andrew Robert Angus)

FAMILY TREE

MICHAEL (*DAD*), UNA (*MUM*)
|
NATURAL
LESLEY, DUNCAN, STUART (*DIED*), CAROLINE
|

ANDY (SIMON)
ALISTAIR (IAN)

|
NATURAL
JILL, CLARE, STEPHEN
|
RAY, AUDREY/SALLY
|
DIVORCED
AUDREY/SALLY
NO OTHER CHILDREN
|
RAY, **MARRIED** CAROLE
|
NATURAL
JAMES, LOUISA